WHAT IS LIFE ABOUT?

THE LIFE BOOK

twitter.com/thelifebook
facebook.com/thelifebookmovement

WHAT IS THE LIFE BOOK?

PART 1

Part 1 is God's story before Jesus shows up on the scene. It's a quick re-telling of the first part of the Bible before Jesus arrives. It explains how things were great, then went bad and why Jesus has to come make things right.

PART 2

Part 2 is straight from the Bible. It's the story of Jesus while He was on Earth. He does some amazing stuff.

WHAT ABOUT YOU?

This part is about what God's story means for your life. What does Jesus have to do with you? What is your role in the world God created? What does God want from you?

HELP!

This part gives some help and answers for things you or your friends might be struggling with. The Bible is full of good answers and guidance for tough stuff in life. It's God's advice, so it has to be pretty good.

STUDENT NOTES

Four students make notes and ask questions all through The Life Book.
(Free Clue: You can tell each student apart by their handwriting.)

DYLAN

I'm 17. Not really into spiritual stuff, but open-minded. Love gaming and science fiction. When I graduate, I want to design the first mass produced flying car.

I hate it when people are fake. I love asking questions and trying to figure things out. My dog's name is Buster. I spend most of my time hanging with Jake Foster doing stupid stuff.

TAYLOR (TAY)

15 yrs old. I'm just a girl who loves God and hope you do too! I want to help others learn more about Jesus. Maybe be a missionary or something like that, so I can tell others how much God loves them. I hope my notes help you. I love helping people and hate it when people are mean.
I play guitar, piano and sing but I'm not sure if I'm any good.

PEDRO (A.K.A. PB)

Freshman this year. Friends call me PB because I put peanut butter on everything. Love sports and am pretty good at them. Hope to play professional football when I get older. Still trying to figure out God and stuff. My girlfriend tells me about Him.

Moved to a new school this year. Hope to start at quarterback. I hate sitting on the bench. I don't get people who don't like sports.

Spend a lot of time with my girlfriend. I pretty much hate homework.

VANESSA

Just turned 16. Love guys. Wish life wasn't so messed up.
I want to be a singer someday. Go to church every week, but it's not a big deal, just something mom and I do together.
Kinda interested in what God is all about. Hate it when people talk about me behind my back. Love knowing all the gossip.
Dream a lot. Just waiting for the man of my dreams to become real.

ADULT NOTES

UNCLE G. (A.K.A. GIDEON WILLIAMS)

I'm the old guy, but I love God and love teens. Those who know me call me Uncle G. I grew up in the 'hood' as they call it. Thanks to my mom I made it through. And thanks to my grandma, I became a follower of Jesus. I'm just here to put in my two cents.

I still don't understand everything about God and the Bible, but I hope I can help a little bit. They say my gray hair gives me wisdom. I don't know about that, but I do know that I've tried to learn as much as I can through the years. So, I hope I can help you get to know God and Jesus better.

PART 1

THE STORY OF GOD AND PEOPLE
(quick retelling of the first part of the Bible)

GOD MAKES IT ALL
(read more in Genesis, the first book in the Bible)

Before time began (as we know it), God existed. That seems tough to
understand, but God was and is and will always be. I guess when you are God,
you don't have to explain it all.

I want that kind of power -D

As God, He didn't need to make anything, but He decided to make the universe
and put people on earth. He spoke and everything was created. No magic, no
illusions, just a word followed by a world.

IT'S ALL GOOD
(read more in Genesis Chapter 2)

In the Bible, God says that everything He made was good. From massive galaxies
soaked with shiny stars to tiny molecules packed with DNA, it was all good.
As part of creating our world, God made a man named Adam and a woman
named Eve. What is really cool is that the Bible says God made them in His
image. We don't know exactly what God looks like because the Bible says He is
a spirit, but we do know that He made humans in His likeness. God has the power
to create and He made us creative too. Being made in His image, we also have
the power to love and reason, dream and desire.

*I really wish
everything was
still ALL good. Things
are pretty messed
up. -V*

It's pretty cool when you think about it. We may not be all-wise, all-powerful,
and perfect in every way, but God did make us like Him in some ways. God is not
just some uncaring ruler who runs things from a distance, blessing and punishing
people. He actually cares about the people He made.

Cool thought. -PB

In the Garden of Eden where God placed Adam and Eve, there was no death or suffering, no sin or sadness. Complete trust of each other and God brought pure joy to every moment. God gave them everything they needed and it was a perfect relationship. They were free to do anything except eat the fruit from one special tree.

Can't imagine -PB

EVIL VILLAIN SHOWS UP
(read more in Genesis Chapter 3)

Totally hate snakes! - Tay

Snakes can't be trusted. Satan (an angel who was kicked out of heaven when he tried to take over) basically told Adam and Eve that God was lying to them and that they shouldn't trust Him. Satan told them that God didn't want them eating from the special tree because He was just trying to keep them from becoming like Him. He also told them God was bluffing on the punishment, which was death.

I know what it's like to make bad choices when it comes to trust. -V ♡

Adam and Eve thought it over, trashed their trust of God, chose to trust the snake Satan and took a bite that would change the world. In that one bite, trust was shattered, and the relationship between God and Adam and Eve was broken. As a result, evil (sin) entered into the perfect world.

Really? One bite and the whole human race has to pay? -D

THE CURSE

A curse fell on Adam and Eve as well as all who would come after them. Now the perfect world would be messy and full of struggle, pain, suffering and shame. Because of their sin, death entered the world. Plants, animals, Adam and Eve, and all their offspring would live for a while and then die. There was no longer the possibility of a close relationship with God. He had to kick them out of the perfect Garden of Eden, and He would no longer walk with them, talk with them, or be close with them as He had before. Sin was now between them.

> Just never thought of my sin and stuff as a big deal.
> -PB

MURDER

The curse of sin and evil in the world showed its ugly head when Adam and Eve's son Cain killed his brother Abel. For many, many years, evil ruled on the earth until God decided it was time to start over.

DO-OVER

God found one man who was living right and chose him to start everything all over. He asked Noah to build a huge boat that would survive a world-wide flood. In this huge boat, Noah took his family and a pair of each animal so they could repopulate the earth.

> Glad I wasn't Noah. Build a boat in the desert? No way. -V

The flood came and the world was wiped out, except for the people and the animals on the huge boat. They started over.

STARTING AGAIN

Because the flood did not break the curse, sin and rebellion against God's ways started all over again. God started a new nation by making a huge promise to

His chosen leader named Abraham. He told Abraham that he would be the father of many nations. Oh, by the way, Abraham and his wife Sarah were really old when God made this promise.

I remember this part of the Bible. Sarah laughed when Abraham told her. — Tay

I saw the Joseph musical on Broadway with my aunt. Didn't he have a colored coat or something like that? - V

Eventually Isaac (Abraham and Sarah's son) was born and became a leader of God's people. Isaac had a son named Jacob (who was quite a schemer). Jacob moved his family to Egypt to escape a famine and to be with his son named Joseph, who stayed faithful to God even though he went through a bunch of bad stuff like slavery and prison. God used Joseph to save His family.

Science check. Okay, how does that happen? On fire, but not burning? I guess if you believe God made everything, then He can mess with scientific laws whenever he wants. - D

SLAVERY

For about 400 years, God's people lived as slaves in Egypt. Until . . . God lit up a bush in the desert. God signed up Moses as the next leader by speaking to him through a burning bush (the bush was on fire, but not burning up) in the desert.

Plague = bad stuff! Water turning to blood, frogs everywhere, disease, locusts, darkness, etc. Bad stuff! — Tay

Moses asked Pharaoh to set God's people free from slavery. Pharaoh refused and God sent a nasty plague. Moses kept asking — Pharaoh kept refusing — God kept sending plagues on Egypt. You'd think Pharaoh would get the message. One final request, one final denial and then God sent the worst plague of all.

Glad he wasn't leading my country. - PB

PASSING OVER

Before God sent the last plague (death of the firstborn from every family), He gave Moses some specific directions to save the lives of His people. (God seems to always provide a way to be saved from terrible <u>consequences.</u>) God told Moses to have each family kill a lamb and smear the lamb's blood over the top of the door to their house.

True! — Tay

When the plague came, all of God's people were saved but the firstborn of each Egyptian family died. Pharaoh gave in and decided to set God's people free.

That's really sad. Seems unfair for the Egyptians to die just because Pharaoh was a jerk. — V

They took off only to have Pharaoh change his mind and follow them. With the Red Sea in front of them and Pharaoh's army behind them, God miraculously parted the sea. God's people crossed over, the sea moved back into place and they finally tasted freedom.

And Pharaoh's army drowned of the movie. — PB   saw part

10 LAWS

Free from slavery, God gave Moses 10 laws that would help His people live in such a way that God would be honored and their society would work. The laws were not given to punish them, but every law had a good purpose to help God's people live together well and have a relationship with God.

Never thought about God's laws like that. — V

Some of the laws were about not worshipping <u>idols,</u> not stealing, lying, and stuff like that.

I think maybe we still turn to idols. Forgive me. — Tay

Instead of following the ten commandments, many of God's people turned to idols and other gods. Because the curse was still in effect, people also ignored some of the other laws. God's laws didn't break the curse, but when people broke His laws, it was just more evidence that the curse was real and it was strong.

BLOOD PAYMENT

Unfortunately, the laws were broken often. So God gave His people a plan to pay for their law breaking. Because blood is the source of life for all, God's plan for payment involved the spilling of blood (kind of like when He protected His people from the final plague in Egypt).

Animals were to be sacrificed as payment for sin and wrong doing. The curse could not be broken by these sacrifices, but the blood of an animal would provide temporary cover from God's punishment of their sin.

Kind of weird to think that blood somehow made up for sin. I guess it makes more sense of Jesus being killed. – PB

I know it sounds strange, but I sometimes feel the pull of this curse – V

The curse still reigned in the world — the curse that entered the world because of Adam and Eve's decision to choose to trust Satan instead of God still reigned in the world.

THE PROMISE

Through His people, God began to share the promise of one who would come and break the curse once and for all. A Messiah, a leader, a Savior was coming who would fix the relationship between humans and God. This Savior would not only show us a new way to live, but He would also be the final sacrifice — his blood paying the penalty for all sin.

Remember: sin equals death and the Bible refers to death as hell (being punished forever). Someone would have to pay for our sin. Without a Savior, the result of our sin is eternal punishment. You might say we were on a highway to hell. The promised Savior would provide us a way to avoid being punished forever. *Amazing when I think about it. Thank You Jesus for breaking the curse. — Tay*

Oh, so he took our place? - PB

*Yes! - Uncle G

The blood of animals covered sin before Jesus showed up, but the only way to finally break the curse once and for all was to have a perfect sacrifice. According to those who told about His coming, the promised Savior would live a life without any sin. He would be absolutely perfect. But in a strange twist of events, He would offer His innocent life and pure blood as a (final sacrifice) by allowing people to kill Him. His blood would pay the penalty for all sin.

So that's why Jesus died? I had no idea -D

THE HOPE

When the Savior comes, all who chose to believe (trust) that His final sacrifice really did break the curse, would have the curse broken in their own life.* They would be made right with God and all of their sin would be forgiven. They would become followers of this Savior, living like He lived and helping others come to trust in His ways.

See my note on the next page.

JESUS CHRIST SHOWS UP

Part 2 is all about the promised one, Jesus Christ, showing up. Jesus comes as the eternal Son of God in human form to forever break the curse. He was fully divine and fully human. His own people (God's chosen people) rejected Him, yet He lived a pure life without sin, and because of this, he became the perfect sacrifice. He took our place, spilling His own blood as the final sacrifice to break the curse. Miraculously proving He was God's eternal son, God raised Him from the dead.

Here is the true story of Jesus that forever changed the world and just maybe your life . . .

* That's what it was like for me. I was sixteen and headed the wrong way when some older guy gave me a little green Bible in the detention center. I read it because I didn't have anything else to do and he seemed different, like he actually cared about me. I didn't understand a lot of what the Bible said, but I did realize that I was messed up and needed a new start. There was a section in the back that talked about being forgiven and following Jesus. I prayed the prayer they had in there and my life began to change. Not sure what happened except that God got hold of me and started making changes. I wish I could find the guy who gave me that Bible and thank him. Because of him my sins are forgiven, I am living the life God wants for me and I am going to heaven when I die.

- Uncle G.

PART 2

THE STORY OF JESUS COMING TO EARTH
(The REAL Bible as God gave it to us)

BOOK OF JOHN
(straight from the Bible)

Not trying to seem like I know everything, but I learned that the WORD is Jesus. - Tay

In the beginning was the Word, and the Word was with God, and the Word was God. He was in the beginning with God. All things were made through him, and without him was not any thing made that was made. In him was life, and the life was the light of men. The light shines in the darkness, and the darkness has not overcome it.

There was a man sent from God, whose name was John. He came as a witness, to bear witness about the light, that all might believe through him. He was not the light, but came to bear witness about the light.

The true light, which enlightens everyone, was coming into the world. He was in the world, and the world was made through him, yet the world did not know him. He came to his own, and his own people did not receive him. But to all who did receive him, who believed in his name, he gave the right to become children of God, who were born, not of blood nor of the will of the flesh nor of the will of man, but of God.

Rejected by his own people? Harsh! - PB

Pretty cool that Jesus leaves heaven for earth. - V

And the Word became flesh and dwelt among us, and we have seen his glory, glory as of the only Son from the Father, full of grace and truth. (John bore witness about him, and cried out, "This was he of whom I said, "He who comes after me ranks before me, because he was before me.") And from his fullness we have all received, grace upon grace. For the law was given through Moses; grace and truth came through Jesus Christ.

No one has ever seen God; the only God, who is at the Father's side, he has made him known.

The Testimony of John the Baptist

And this is the testimony of John, when the Jews sent priests and Levites from Jerusalem to ask him, "Who are you?" He confessed, and did not deny, but confessed, "I am not the Christ." And they asked him, "What then? Are you Elijah?" He said, "I am not." "Are you the Prophet?" And he answered, "No." So they said to him, "Who are you? We need to give an answer to those who sent us. What do you say about yourself?"

Man, they are drilling the guy. – D

Felt like that before, except no o was listening. – Tay

He said, "I am the voice of one crying out in the wilderness, 'Make straight the way of the Lord,'" as the prophet Isaiah said." (Now they had been sent from the Pharisees.) They asked him, "Then why are you baptizing, if you are neither the Christ, nor Elijah, nor the Prophet?"

Not sure I get the whole baptism thing. – PB

John answered them, "I baptize with water, but among you stands one you do not know, even he who comes after me, the strap of whose sandal I am not worthy to untie." These things took place in Bethany across the Jordan, where John was baptizing.*

* When I was just a boy, momma would give me a bath every night because I would get all dirty playing in the abandoned lot next to where we lived. Every night she would tell me about how water makes us new and fresh again. No matter how dirty I got, she always made me clean. So baptism reminds me of that. – Uncle G.

The Lamb of God

The next day he saw Jesus coming toward him, and said, "Behold, the Lamb of God, who takes away the sin of the world! This is he of whom I said, 'After me comes a man who ranks before me, because he was before me.' I myself did not know him, but for this purpose I came baptizing with water, that he might be revealed to Israel."

That would be cool to see. People probably freaked. – V

And John bore witness: "I saw the Spirit descend from heaven like a dove, and it remained on him. I myself did not know him, but he who sent me to baptize with water said to me, 'He on whom you see the Spirit descend and remain, this is he who baptizes with the Holy Spirit.' And I have seen and have borne witness that this is the Son of God."

Jesus Calls the First Disciples

The next day again John was standing with two of his disciples, and he looked at Jesus as he walked by and said, "Behold, the Lamb of God!" The two disciples heard him say this, and they followed Jesus. Jesus turned and saw them following and said to them, "What are you seeking?" And they said to him, "Rabbi" (which means Teacher), "where are you staying?" He said to them, "Come and you will see." So they came and saw where he was staying, and they stayed with him that day, for it was about the tenth hour.

Jesus loves to ask lots of ????s. – Tay

One of the two who heard John speak and followed Jesus was Andrew, Simon Peter's brother. He first found his own brother Simon and said to him, "We have found the Messiah" (which means Christ). He brought him to Jesus. Jesus looked at him and said, "So you are Simon the son of John? You shall be called Cephas" (which means Peter).

Wonder what name Jesus would give me? – V

Jesus Calls Philip and Nathanael

The next day Jesus decided to go to Galilee. He found Philip and said to him, "Follow me." Now Philip was from Bethsaida, the city of Andrew and Peter. Philip found Nathanael and said to him, "We have found him of whom Moses in the Law and also the prophets wrote, Jesus of Nazareth, the son of Joseph." Nathanael said to him, "Can anything good come out of Nazareth?" Philip said to him, "Come and see." Jesus saw Nathanael coming toward him and said of him, "Behold, an Israelite indeed, in whom there is no deceit!" Nathanael said to him, "How do you know me?" Jesus answered him, "Before Philip called you, when you were under the fig tree, I saw you." Nathanael answered him, "Rabbi, you are the Son of God! You are the King of Israel!" Jesus answered him, "Because I said to you, 'I saw you under the fig tree,' do you believe? You will see greater things than these." And he said to him, "Truly, truly, I say to you, you will see heaven opened, and the angels of God ascending and descending on the Son of Man."

CHAPTER 2

Turning Water into Wine

On the third day there was a wedding at Cana in Galilee, and the mother of Jesus was there. Jesus also was invited to the wedding with his disciples. When the wine ran out, the mother of Jesus said to him, "They have no wine." And Jesus said to her, "Woman, what does this have to do with me? My hour has not yet come." His mother said to the servants, "Do whatever he tells you." Now there were six stone water jars there for the Jewish rites of purification, each holding twenty or thirty gallons. Jesus said to the servants, "Fill the jars with water." And they filled them up to the brim. And he said to them, "Now

Are you stalking me? LOL - D

draw some out and take it to the master of the feast." So they took it. When the master of the feast tasted the water now become wine, and did not know where it came from (though the servants who had drawn the water knew), the master of the feast called the bridegroom and said to him, "Everyone serves the good wine first, and when people have drunk freely, then the poor wine. But you have kept the good wine until now." This, the first of his signs, Jesus did at Cana in Galilee, and manifested his glory. And his disciples believed in him.

After this he went down to Capernaum, with his mother and his brothers and his disciples, and they stayed there for a few days.

Okay, let me get this straight: 1. Jesus is at a party 2. He is making wine. Hmmm... totally different than the Jesus I've heard about. K. Got me thinking. – PB

Jesus Cleanses the Temple

The Passover of the Jews was at hand, and Jesus went up to Jerusalem. In the temple he found those who were selling oxen and sheep and pigeons, and the money-changers sitting there. And making a whip of cords, he drove them all out of the temple, with the sheep and oxen. And he poured out the coins of the money-changers and overturned their tables. And he told those who sold the pigeons,

Cool. Never knew Jesus got ticked off. So much for the meek little teacher. – D

"Take these things away; do not make my Father's house a house of trade." His disciples remembered that it was written, "Zeal for your house will consume me."

So the Jews said to him, "What sign do you show us for doing these things?" Jesus answered them, "Destroy this temple, and in three days I will raise it up." The Jews then said, "It has taken forty-six years to build this temple, and will you raise it up in three days?" But he was speaking about the temple of his body. When therefore he was raised from the dead, his disciples remembered

Jesus seems to confuse people a lot. – V

that he had said this, and they believed the Scripture and the word that Jesus had spoken.

Jesus Knows What Is in Man

Now when he was in Jerusalem at the Passover Feast, many believed in his name when they saw the signs that he was doing. But Jesus on his part did not entrust himself to them, because he knew all people and needed no one to bear witness about man, for he himself knew what was in man.

Wish all my friends and family would start to believe in Jesus. — Tay

CHAPTER 3

You Must Be Born Again

Now there was a man of the Pharisees named Nicodemus, a ruler of the Jews. This man came to Jesus by night and said to him, "Rabbi, we know that you are a teacher come from God, for no one can do these signs that you do unless God is with him."

Wonder what its like sneaking around at night in one of those robe things. Funny. — D

Jesus answered him, "Truly, truly, I say to you, unless one is born again he cannot see the kingdom of God."

I definitely want to see the kingdom of God! — Tay

Nicodemus said to him, "How can a man be born when he is old? Can he enter a second time into his mother's womb and be born?"

Don't even want to think about that. — V

Jesus answered, "Truly, truly, I say to you, unless one is born of water and the Spirit, he cannot enter the kingdom of God. That which is born of the flesh is flesh, and that which is born of the Spirit is spirit. Do not marvel that I said to you, 'You must be born again.' The wind blows where it wishes, and you hear its sound, but you do not know where it comes from or where it goes. So it is with everyone who is born of the Spirit."

Nicodemus said to him, "How can these things be?"

I'm with you Nic. I'd be asking the same thing! - PB

Jesus answered him, "Are you the teacher of Israel and yet you do not understand these things? Truly, truly, I say to you, we speak of what we know, and bear witness to what we have seen, but you do not receive our testimony. If I have told you earthly things and you do not believe, how can you believe if I tell you heavenly things? No one has ascended into heaven except he who descended from heaven, the Son of Man. And as Moses lifted up the serpent in the wilderness, so must the Son of Man be lifted up, that whoever believes in him may have eternal life.

Snakes again? - Tay

For God So Loved the World

"For God so loved the world, that he gave his only Son, that whoever believes in him should not perish but have eternal life.

Saw a guy at a pro football game with a big sign that said this. - PB

"For God did not send his Son into the world to condemn the world, but in order that the world might be saved through him. Whoever believes in him is not condemned, but whoever does not believe is condemned already, because he has not believed in the name of the only Son of God. And this is the judgment: the light has come into the world, and people loved the darkness rather than the light because their works were evil.

I didn't know that. Condemned already for not believing? Does that mean I'm going to hell if I don't believe in Jesus? - D

I know people like that. - V

"For everyone who does wicked things hates the light and does not come to the light, lest his works should be exposed. But whoever does what is true comes to the light, so that it may be clearly seen that his works have been carried out in God."

* Hell? Jesus talks a whole bunch about it. Did Jesus just make it up to scare people? No, it's real. It may seem unfair to be condemned already (on a highway to hell) for not believing, but we all deserve it because we rebel against God by doing our own thing and breaking His rules. We are all born with the curse of sin. The result of that curse is hell – punishment forever. Everyone who does not believe in who Jesus is and what He has done for them will experience the lake of fire Jesus talks about. BUT – don't forget – God provides a way to be with Him forever in heaven. Believe in Jesus just like He said. So, I guess the most loving thing I can do for you is tell you how you can avoid hell and spend forever in heaven.

– Uncle G.

John the Baptist Exalts Christ

After this Jesus and his disciples went into the Judean countryside, and he remained there with them and was baptizing. John also was baptizing at Aenon near Salim, because water was plentiful there, and people were coming and being baptized (for John had not yet been put in prison).

Prison? Must be coming up. - PB

Now a discussion arose between some of John's disciples and a Jew over purification. And they came to John and said to him, "Rabbi, he who was with you across the Jordan, to whom you bore witness—look, he is baptizing, and all are going to him." John answered, "A person cannot receive even one thing unless it is given him from heaven. You yourselves bear me witness, that I said, 'I am not the Christ, but I have been sent before him.' The one who has the bride is the bridegroom. The friend of the bridegroom, who stands and hears him, rejoices greatly at the bridegroom's voice. Therefore this joy of mine is now complete. He must increase, but I must decrease."

Decrease? I guess it means God gets more attention and I get less? Honestly that's a tough thing for me I love attention

He who comes from above is above all. He who is of the earth belongs to the earth and speaks in an earthly way. He who comes from heaven is above all. He bears witness to what he has seen and heard, yet no one receives his testimony. Whoever receives his testimony sets his seal to this, that God is true. For he whom God has sent utters the words of God, for he gives the Spirit without measure. The Father loves the Son and has given all things into his hand. Whoever believes in the Son has eternal life; whoever does not obey the Son shall not see life, but the wrath of God remains on him.

There it is again - don't believe = punishment Hmmm - D

CHAPTER 4

Jesus and the Woman of Samaria

Now when Jesus learned that the Pharisees had heard that Jesus was making and baptizing more disciples than John (although Jesus himself did not baptize, but only his disciples), he left Judea and departed again for Galilee. And he had to pass through Samaria. So he came to a town of Samaria called Sychar, near the field that Jacob had given to his son Joseph. Jacob's well was there; so Jesus, wearied as he was from his journey, was sitting beside the well. It was about the sixth hour. A woman from Samaria came to draw water. Jesus said to her, "Give me a drink." (For his disciples had gone away into the city to buy food.) The Samaritan woman said to him, "How is it that you, a Jew, ask for a drink from me, a woman of Samaria?" (For Jews have no dealings with Samaritans.)

→ Jesus doesn't seem to care about stupid rules. I like that. – PB

Jesus answered her, "If you knew the gift of God, and who it is that is saying to you, 'Give me a drink,' you would have asked him, and he would have given you living water." The woman said to him, "Sir, you have nothing to draw water with, and the well is deep. Where do you get that living water? Are you greater than our father Jacob? He gave us the well and drank from it himself, as did his sons and his livestock."

Living water? – V

Jesus said to her, "Everyone who drinks of this water will be thirsty again, but whoever drinks of the water that I will give him will never be thirsty again. The water that I will give him will become in him a spring of water welling up to eternal life." The woman said to him, "Sir, give me this water, so that I will not

Now it makes sense. Living water means eternal life. – V

be thirsty or have to come here to draw water."

Jesus said to her, "Go, call your husband, and come here." The woman answered him, "I have no husband." Jesus said to her, "You are right in saying, 'I have no husband'; for you have had five husbands, and the one you now have is not your husband. What you have said is true." The woman said to him, "Sir, I perceive that you are a prophet. Our fathers worshiped on this mountain, but you say that in Jerusalem is the place where people ought to worship."

> Man! He knows everything about everybody. PB

Jesus said to her, "Woman, believe me, the hour is coming when neither on this mountain nor in Jerusalem will you worship the Father. You worship what you do not know; we worship what we know, for salvation is from the Jews. But the hour is coming, and is now here, when the true worshipers will worship the Father in spirit and truth, for the Father is seeking such people to worship him. God is spirit, and those who worship him must worship in spirit and truth." The woman said to him, "I know that Messiah is coming (he who is called Christ). When he comes, he will tell us all things." Jesus said to her, "I who speak to you am he."*

* Big point. Jesus says He is the promised Messiah. That's a huge claim. — Uncle G.

Just then his disciples came back. They marveled that he was talking with a woman, but no one said, "What do you seek?" or, "Why are you talking with her?" So the woman left her water jar and went away into town and said to the people, "Come, see a man who told me all that I ever did. Can this be the Christ?" They went out of the town and were coming to him.

Story was too juicy not to tell everyone too! — V

Meanwhile the disciples were urging him, saying, "Rabbi, eat." But he said to them, "I have food to eat that you do not know about." So the disciples said to one another, "Has anyone brought him something to eat?" Jesus said to them, "My food is to do the will of him who sent me and to accomplish his work. Do you not say, 'There are yet four months, then comes the harvest'? Look, I tell you, lift up your eyes, and see that the fields are white for harvest. Already the one who reaps is receiving wages and gathering fruit for eternal life, so that sower and reaper may rejoice together. For here the saying holds true, 'One sows and another reaps.' I sent you to reap that for which you did not labor. Others have labored, and you have entered into their labor."

He loves to twist things-:)

Good because I'm starving. - PB

Many Samaritans from that town believed in him because of the woman's testimony, "He told me all that I ever did." So when the Samaritans came to him, they asked him to stay with them, and he stayed there two days. And many more believed because of his word. They said to the woman, "It is no longer because of what you said that we believe, for we have heard for ourselves, and we know that this is indeed the Savior of the world."

Still freaks me out that he knows everything about everyone. - PB

And my savior too! - Tay

After the two days he departed for Galilee. (For Jesus himself had testified that a prophet has no honor in his own hometown.) So when he came to Galilee, the Galileans welcomed him, having seen all that he had done in Jerusalem at the feast. For they too had gone to the feast.

These guys party all the time! - PB

Jesus Heals an Official's Son

So he came again to Cana in Galilee, where he had made the water wine. And at Capernaum there was an official whose son was ill. When this man heard that Jesus had come from Judea to Galilee, he went to him and asked him to come down and heal his son, for he was at the point of death. So Jesus said to him, "Unless you see signs and wonders you will not believe." The official said to him, "Sir, come down before my child dies." Jesus said to him, "Go; your son will live."

beats going to the hospital. – V

The man believed the word that Jesus spoke to him and went on his way. As he was going down, his servants met him and told him that his son was recovering. So he asked them the hour when he began to get better, and they said to him, "Yesterday at the seventh hour the fever left him." The father knew that was the hour when Jesus had said to him, "Your son will live." And he himself believed, and all his <u>household.</u> This was now the second sign that Jesus did when he had come from Judea to Galilee.

Not sure my dad would believe even if he saw Jesus heal that kid. – Tay

CHAPTER 5

The Healing at the Pool on the Sabbath

After this there was a feast of the Jews, and Jesus went up to Jerusalem. Now there is in Jerusalem by the Sheep Gate a pool, in Aramaic called Bethesda, which has five roofed colonnades. In these lay a multitude of invalids—blind, lame, and paralyzed, waiting for the moving of the water, for an angel of the Lord went down at certain seasons into the pool, and stirred the water: whoever stepped in first after the stirring of the water was healed of whatever disease he had.

I wonder if an angel still goes down to that pool today. – V

One man was there who had been an invalid for thirty-eight years. When Jesus saw him lying <u>there and knew that</u> he had already been there a long time, he said to him, "Do you want to be healed?" The sick man answered him, "Sir, I have no one to put me into the pool when the water is stirred up, and while I am going another steps down before me."

Some days I'd much rather stay home sick from school than to get better and have to go. – D

Jesus said to him, "Get up, take up your bed, and walk." And at once the man was healed, and he took up his bed and walked.

For real – if I saw that happen I think I'd want to follow Jesus around just to see what he was going to do next. – PB

Now that day was the <u>Sabbath</u>. So the Jews said to the man who had been healed, "It is the Sabbath, and it is not lawful for you to take up your bed." But he answered them, "The man who healed me, that man said to me, 'Take up your bed, and walk.'" They asked him, "Who is the man who said to you, 'Take up your bed and walk'?" Now the man who had been healed did not know who it was, for Jesus had withdrawn, as there was a crowd in the place. Afterward Jesus found him in the temple and said to him, "See, you are well! Sin no more, that nothing worse may happen to you." The man went away and told the Jews that it was Jesus who had healed him.

That's the day we're supposed to rest. It's one of the 10 commandments. – Tay

Pretty sure you couldn't slip away today. The news would be all over this stuff. – D

Seems like a stupid rule! – PB

And this was why the Jews were persecuting Jesus, because he was doing these things on the Sabbath. But Jesus answered them, "My Father is working until now, and I am working."

Jesus Is Equal with God

This was why the Jews were seeking all the more to kill him, because not only was he breaking the Sabbath, but he was even calling God his own Father, making himself equal with God.

I could see how that would make them nervous – D

The Authority of the Son

So Jesus said to them, "Truly, truly, I say to you, the Son can do nothing of his own accord, but only what he sees the Father doing. For whatever the Father does, that the Son does likewise. For the Father loves the Son and shows him all that he himself is doing. And greater works than these will he show him, so that

The Life Book…Got Questions? Ask the person who gave you The Life Book you may marvel. For as the Father raises the dead and gives them life, so also the Son gives life to whom he will. The Father judges no one, but has given all judgment to the Son, that all may honor the Son, just as they honor the Father. Whoever does not honor the Son does not honor the Father who sent him."

Can't imagine that kind of power. - PB

*Growing up we used to go to my Grandma's house every Sunday afternoon. We'd just sit around doing nothing but talking, except for when it was time for sweets. (Grandma made this amazing apple pie with cinnamon and homemade ice cream on top.) But my momma would always say we needed our Sabbath rest 'cause that's the way God made us.' Keeping the Sabbath day holy is one of the 10 commandments and Jesus talks more about it. In the Bible in the book of Mark, chapter 2 verse 27 Jesus says that the Sabbath was made for man to make sure we got regular rest and a day set apart for God. Seems like the religious leaders in Jesus' time took it a little too far.

- Uncle G.

"Truly, truly, I say to you, whoever hears my word and <u>believes</u> him who sent me has eternal life. He does not come into judgment, but has passed from death to life.

I see people who say they believe in Jesus but don't live like it. Seems like believing should change everything. — Tay

"Truly, truly, I say to you, an hour is coming, and is now here, when the dead will hear the voice of the Son of God, and those who hear will live. For as the Father has life in himself, so he has granted the Son also to have life in himself. And he has given him authority to execute judgment, because he is the Son of Man. Do not marvel at this, for an hour is coming when all who are in the tombs will hear his voice and come out, those who have done good to the resurrection of life, and those who have done evil to the resurrection of judgment.

scary – V

Witnesses to Jesus
"I can do nothing on my own. As I hear, I judge, and my judgment is just, because I seek not my own will but the will of him who sent me. If I alone bear witness about myself, my testimony is not deemed true.

"There is another who bears witness about me, and I know that the testimony that he bears about me is true. You sent to John, and he has borne witness to the truth. Not that the testimony that I receive is from man, but I say these things so that you may be saved.

"He was a burning and shining lamp, and you were willing to rejoice for a while in his light. But the testimony that I have is greater than that of John. For the works that the Father has given me to accomplish, the very works that I am doing, bear witness about me that the Father has sent me. And the Father who sent me has himself borne witness about me.

"His voice you have never heard, his form you have never seen, and you do not have his word abiding in you, for you do not believe the one whom he has sent. You search the Scriptures because you think that in them you have eternal life; and it is they that bear witness about me, yet you refuse to come to me that you may have life.

Jesus is like, "Hello, I'm right here. The one you've been waiting for. — Tay

"I do not receive glory from people. But I know that you do not have the love of God within you. I have come in my Father's name, and you do not receive me. If another comes in his own name, you will receive him. How can you believe, when you receive glory from one another and do not seek the glory that comes from the only God? Do not think that I will accuse you to the Father. There is one who accuses you: Moses, on whom you have set your hope. For if you believed Moses, you would believe me; for he wrote of me. But if you do not believe his writings, how will you believe my words?"

Didn't know Jesus went off on people like that. — V

CHAPTER 6

Jesus Feeds the Five Thousand

After this Jesus went away to the other side of the Sea of Galilee, which is the Sea of Tiberias. And a large crowd was following him, because they saw the signs that he was doing on the sick. Jesus went up on the mountain, and there he sat down with his disciples. Now the Passover, the feast of the Jews, was at hand.

Sounds much better than going to my boring church. — V

Lifting up his eyes, then, and seeing that a large crowd was coming toward him, Jesus said to Philip, "Where are we to buy bread, so that these people may eat?" He said this to test him, for he himself knew what he would do. Philip answered him, "Two hundred denarii would not buy enough bread for each of them to get a little." One of his disciples, Andrew, Simon Peter's brother, said to him, "There is a boy here who has five barley loaves and two fish, but what are they for so many?" Jesus said, "Have the people sit down." Now there was much grass in the place. So the men sat down, about five thousand in number.

Jesus then took the loaves, and when he had given thanks, he distributed them to those who were seated. So also the fish, as much as they wanted. And when they had eaten their fill, he told his disciples, "Gather up the leftover fragments, that nothing may be lost." So they gathered them up and filled twelve baskets with fragments from the five barley loaves left by those who had eaten. When the people saw the sign that he had done, they said, "This is indeed the Prophet who is to come into the world!" Perceiving then that they were about to come and take him by force to make him king, Jesus withdrew again to the mountain by himself.

Jesus Walks on Water

When evening came, his disciples went down to the sea, got into a boat, and started across the sea to Capernaum. It was now dark, and Jesus had not yet come to them. The sea became rough because a strong wind was blowing.

When they had rowed about three or four miles, they saw Jesus walking on the sea and coming near the boat, and they were frightened. But he said to them,

Handwritten margin notes:

Hate tests! — V ♡

Not sure I get how this happened. So, did the fish and bread just keep multiplying right in front of the people or what? Wonder what it looked like. — PB

Big lunch for 1 boy. — D

* The Jewish people (God's people) thought the Messiah was going to be their king here on earth. Kind of like if we saw someone doing amazing things we might want to make him our president. — Uncle G.

"It is I; do not be afraid." Then they were glad to take him into the boat, and immediately the boat was at the land to which they were going.

I would've been scared too! Must be cool to walk on water though. – V

I Am the Bread of Life

On the next day the crowd that remained on the other side of the sea saw that there had been only one boat there, and that Jesus had not entered the boat with his disciples, but that his disciples had gone away alone. Other boats from Tiberias came near the place where they had eaten the bread after the Lord had given thanks. So when the crowd saw that Jesus was not there, nor his disciples, they themselves got into the boats and went to Capernaum, seeking Jesus.

When they found him on the other side of the sea, they said to him, "Rabbi, when did you come here?"

Jesus answered them, "Truly, truly, I say to you, you are seeking me, not because you saw signs, but because you ate your fill of the loaves. Do not labor for the food that perishes, but for the food that endures to eternal life, which the Son of Man will give to you. For on him God the Father has set his seal."

You're suming for the FREE FOOD! – PB

How can we get in on this doing miracles thing? Could make some big bucks with that kind of power. – D

Then they said to him, "What must we do, to be doing the works of God?" Jesus answered them, "This is the work of God, that you believe in him whom he has sent."

I don't get these people. He just made bread and fish appear to feed over 5,000 people and they still don't believe him? What's up with that? – Tay

So they said to him, "Then what sign do you do, that we may see and believe you? What work do you perform? Our fathers ate the manna in the wilderness; as it is written, 'He gave them bread from heaven to eat.'"

Jesus then said to them, "Truly, truly, I say to you, it was not Moses who gave you the bread from heaven, but my Father gives you the true bread from heaven. For the bread of God is he who comes down from heaven and gives life to the world." They said to him, "Sir, give us this bread always."

Big promises - never hungry or thirsty. But I guess he did just feed a ton of people. - D

Jesus said to them, "I am the bread of life; whoever comes to me shall not (hunger) and whoever believes in me shall never thirst. But I said to you that you have seen me and yet do not believe. All that the Father gives me will come to me, and whoever comes to me I will never cast out. For I have come down from heaven, not to do my own will but the will of him who sent me. And this is the will of him who sent me, that I should lose nothing of all that he has given me, but raise it up on the last day. For this is the will of my Father, that everyone who looks on the Son and believes in him should have eternal life, and I will raise him up on the last day."

God's will in a nutshell. - Tay

So the Jews grumbled about him, because he said, "I am the bread that came down from heaven." They said, "Is not this Jesus, the son of Joseph, whose father and mother we know? How does he now say, 'I have come down from heaven'?" Jesus answered them, "Do not grumble among yourselves. No one can come to me unless the Father who sent me draws him. And I will raise him up on the last day.

Tough to escape where you come from. Trust me, I know. - PB

"It is written in the Prophets, 'And they will all be taught by God.' Everyone who has heard and learned from the Father comes to me— not that anyone has seen the Father except he who is from God; he has seen the Father. Truly, truly, I say to you, whoever believes has eternal life. I am the bread of life. Your fathers ate the manna in the wilderness, and they died. This is the bread that comes down from heaven, so that one may eat of it and not die. I am the living bread that came down from heaven. If anyone eats of this bread, he will live forever. And the bread that I will give for the life of the world is my flesh."

The Jews then disputed among themselves, saying, "How can this man give us his flesh to eat?" So Jesus said to them, "Truly, truly, I say to you, unless you eat the flesh of the Son of Man and drink his blood, you have no life in you. Whoever feeds on my flesh and drinks my blood has eternal life, and I will raise him up on the last day. For my flesh is true food, and my blood is true drink. Whoever feeds on my flesh and drinks my blood abides in me, and I in him. As the living Father sent me, and I live because of the Father, so whoever feeds on me, he also will live because of me. This is the bread that came down from heaven, not like the bread the fathers ate and died. Whoever feeds on this bread will live <u>forever</u>." Jesus said these things in the synagogue, as he taught at Capernaum.

[handwritten note:] seems gross. Not sure I get what he's talking about here – V

[handwritten note:] I don't think he's talking about literally eating his body and blood, but more like a spiritual way of thinking about it — at least that's what my youth leader said. – Tay

The Words of Eternal Life

When many of his disciples heard it, they said, "This is a hard saying; who can listen to it?" But Jesus, knowing in himself that his disciples were grumbling about this, said to them, "Do you take offense at this? Then what if you were to see the Son of Man ascending to where he was before? It is the Spirit who gives life; the flesh is no help at all. The words that I have spoken to you are spirit and life. But there are some of you who do not believe." (For Jesus knew from the beginning who those were who did not believe, and who it was who would betray him.)

[handwritten note:] Weird to know someone is going to stab you in the back and you still hang out with them. Don't think I could do that. – D

And he said, "This is why I told you that no one can come to me unless it is granted him by the Father."

I love this verse. I try to tell my friends that Jesus is the only one who can give us eternal life. Sometimes they just don't want to listen.
— Tay

After this many of his disciples turned back and no longer walked with him. So Jesus said to the Twelve, "Do you want to go away as well?" Simon Peter answered him, "Lord, to whom shall we go? You have the words of <u>eternal life</u>, and we have believed, and have come to know, that you are the Holy One of God." Jesus answered them, "Did I not choose you, the Twelve? And yet one of you is a devil." He spoke of Judas the son of Simon Iscariot, for he, one of the Twelve, was going to betray him.

CHAPTER 7

Jesus Goes to the Feast

After this Jesus went about in Galilee. He would not go about in Judea, because the Jews were seeking to kill him. Now the Jews' Feast of Booths was at hand. So his brothers said to him, "Leave here and go to Judea, that your disciples also may see the works you are doing. For no one works in secret if he seeks to be known openly. If you do these things, show yourself to the world." <u>For not even his brothers believed in him.</u>

I know what that's like.
— Tay

Jesus said to them, "My time has not yet come, but your time is always here. The world cannot hate you, but it hates me because I testify about it that its works are (evil) You go up to the feast. I am not yet going up to this feast, for my time has not yet fully come." After saying this, he remained in Galilee.

Tells it like it is - which is cool - D

But after his brothers had gone up to the feast, then he also went up, not publicly but in private. The Jews were looking for him at the feast, and saying, "Where is he?" And there was much muttering about him among the people. While some said, "He is a good man," others said, "No, he is leading the people astray." Yet for fear of the Jews no one spoke openly of him.

They seemed to be pretty ticked off with him. - D

Seems like you can't ignore this guy. You either love him or hate him. Still not sure why the Jews didn't like him. Seems like he was doing good stuff. Guess he wasn't their idea of what Messiah was supposed to be like. - PB

About the middle of the feast Jesus went up into the temple and began teaching. The Jews therefore marveled, saying, "How is it that this man has learning, when he has never studied?" So Jesus answered them, "My teaching is not mine, but his who sent me. If anyone's will is to do God's will, he will know whether the teaching is from God or whether I am speaking on my own authority. The one who speaks on his own authority seeks his own glory; but the one who seeks the glory of him who sent him is true, and in him there is no falsehood. Has not Moses given you the law? Yet none of you keeps the law. Why do you seek to kill me?"

Good question! - PB

My grandpa used to say, Don't shift the blame, but always shift the fame. I think that's what Jesus was doing here - shifting the fame to God. - V

The crowd answered, "You have a demon! Who is seeking to kill you?"

Jesus answered them, "I did one work, and you all marvel at it. Moses gave you circumcision (not that it is from Moses, but from the fathers), and you circumcise a man on the Sabbath. If on the Sabbath a man receives circumcision, so that the law of Moses may not be broken, are you angry with me because on the Sabbath I made a man's whole body well? Do not judge by appearances, but judge with right judgment."

Seems like they should want good stuff to happen no matter what day it is. - V

Can This Be the Christ?

Some of the people of Jerusalem therefore said, "Is not this the man whom they seek to kill? And here he is, speaking openly, and they say nothing to him! Can it be that the authorities really know that this is the Christ? But we know where this man comes from, and when the (Christ) appears, no one will know where he comes from."

Did they know he really was the Christ? - D

So Jesus proclaimed, as he taught in the temple, "You know me, and you know where I come from? But I have not come of my own accord. He who sent me is true, and him you do not know. I know him, for I come from him, and he sent me."

Now that is sweet - D

So they were seeking to arrest him, but no one laid a hand on him, because his hour had not yet (come.) Yet many of the people believed in him. They said, "When the Christ appears, will he do more signs than this man has done?"

Officers Sent to Arrest Jesus

The Pharisees heard the crowd muttering these things about him, and the chief priests and Pharisees sent officers to arrest him.

On what charge? Doesn't seem right. - PB

Jesus then said, "I will be with you a little longer, and then I am going to him who sent me. You will seek me and you will not find me. Where I am you cannot come."

The Jews said to one another, "Where does this man intend to go that we will not find him? Does he intend to go to the Dispersion among the Greeks and teach the Greeks? What does he mean by saying, 'You will <u>seek</u> me and you will not find me,' and, 'Where I am you cannot come'?"

Ultimate hide and go seek. - Tay

The Life Book...Got Questions? Ask the person who gave you The Life Book

Rivers of Living Water

On the last day of the feast, the great day, Jesus stood up and cried out, "If anyone thirsts, let him come to me and drink. Whoever believes in me, as the Scripture has said, 'Out of his heart will flow rivers of living water.'" Now this he said about the Spirit, whom those who believed in him were to <u>receive</u>, for as yet the Spirit had not been given, because Jesus was not yet glorified.

I was taught that when I believed in Jesus as my Savior, the Holy Spirit came to live inside of me. — Tay

Division Among the People

When they heard these words, some of the people said, "This really is the Prophet." Others said, "This is the Christ." But some said, "Is the Christ to come from Galilee? Has not the Scripture said that the Christ comes from the offspring of David, and comes from Bethlehem, the village where David was?"

So there was a division among the people over him. Some of them wanted to arrest him, but no one laid hands on him. *So much for peace and unity. Jesus seems to divide everyone more than bring them together. — V*

The officers then came to the chief priests and Pharisees, who said to them, "Why did you not bring him?" The officers answered, "No one ever spoke like this man!" The Pharisees answered them, "Have you also been deceived? Have any of the authorities or the Pharisees believed in him? But this crowd that does not know the law is accursed."

Funny ... the cops don't want to arrest him. — D

Nicodemus, who had gone to him before, and who was one of them, said to them, "Does our law judge a man without first giving him a hearing and learning what he does?" They replied, "Are you from Galilee too? Search and see that no prophet arises from Galilee." *Jesus seems to have these religious leaders freaking out a bit. — V*

CHAPTER 8

The Woman Caught in Adultery

They went each to his own house, but Jesus went to the Mount of Olives.

yummy! Love olives! Hmmm_ that's kind of cheesy I guess_ - V

Early in the morning he came again to the temple. All the people came to him, and he sat down and taught them. The scribes and the Pharisees brought a woman who had been caught in adultery, and placing her in the midst they said to him, "Teacher, this woman has been caught in the act of adultery. Now in the Law Moses commanded us to stone such women. So what do you say?" This they said to test <u>him</u>, that they might have some charge to bring against him.

Don't mess with the Son of God. - Tay

Jesus bent down and wrote with his finger on the ground. And as they continued to ask him, he stood up and said to them, "Let him who is without sin among you be the first to throw a stone at her." And once more he bent down and wrote on the (ground)

Wonder what he was writing. It sure chased them off. Maybe he was listing their sins or something like that. I would take off too if he started listing mine for everyone to see. - D

But when they heard it, they went away one by one, beginning with the older ones, and Jesus was left alone with the woman standing before him. Jesus stood up and said to her, "Woman, where are they? Has no one condemned you?" She said, "No one, Lord." And Jesus said, "Neither do I condemn you; go, and from now on sin no more."

wow! She went from almost being stoned to death, to a new start. I'd love a new start like that. - V

I Am the Light of the World

Again Jesus spoke to them, saying, "I am the light of the world. Whoever follows me will not walk in darkness, but will have the light of life." So the Pharisees said to him, "You are bearing witness about yourself; your testimony is not true."

Jesus answered, "Even if I do bear witness about myself, my testimony is true, for I know where I came from and where I am going, but you do not know where I come from or where I am going. You judge according to the flesh; I judge no one.

"Yet even if I do judge, my judgment is true, for it is not I alone who judge, but I and the Father who sent me. In your Law it is written that the testimony of two people is true. I am the one who bears witness about myself, and the Father who sent me bears witness about me.

Tricky. - D

They said to him therefore, "Where is your Father?" Jesus answered, "You know neither me nor my Father. If you knew me, you would know my Father also." These words he spoke in the treasury, as he taught in the temple; but no one arrested him, because his hour had not yet come.

It keeps saying this... very cool every time. Can't touch me yet! - PB

So he said to them again, "I am going away, and you will seek me, and you will die in your sin. Where I am going, you cannot come." So the Jews said, "Will he kill himself, since he says, 'Where I am going, you cannot come'?" He said to

Sounds like he's saying he's an alien -D

them, "You are from below; I am from above. You are of this world; I am not of this (world.) I told you that you would die in your sins, for unless you believe that I am he you will die in your sins."

It's all about believing again I'm getting the point. - V

Nobody seems to get him
I know the feeling. - V

So they said to him, "Who are you?" Jesus said to them, "Just what I have been telling you from the beginning. I have much to say about you and much to judge, but he who sent me is true, and I declare to the world what I have heard from him."

They did not understand that he had been speaking to them about the Father. So Jesus said to them, "When you have lifted up the Son of Man, then you will know that I am he, and that I do nothing on my own authority, but speak just as the Father taught me. And he who sent me is with me. He has not left me alone, for I always do the things that are pleasing to <u>him</u>." As he was saying these things, many believed in him.

Wish I could say the same. - Tay

The Truth Will Set You Free

Heard this before but didn't know it was Jesus who said it. Seems like he's saying his Word is the truth and that's what sets you free. Different than how I heard it before. -D

So Jesus said to the Jews who had believed in him, "If you abide in my word, you are truly my disciples, and you will know the truth, and the truth will set you (free.) They answered him, "We are offspring of Abraham and have never been enslaved to anyone. How is it that you say, 'You will become free'?" Jesus answered them, "Truly, truly, I say to you, everyone who commits sin is a slave to sin. The slave does not remain in the house forever; the son remains forever. So if the Son sets you free, you will be free indeed. I know that you are offspring of Abraham; yet you seek to kill me because my word finds no place in you. I speak of what I have seen with my Father, and you do what you have heard from your father."

From slave to son - very cool. - V

You Are of Your Father the Devil

They answered him, "Abraham is our father." Jesus said to them, "If you were Abraham's children, you would be doing the works Abraham did, but now you seek to kill me, a man who has told you the truth that I heard from God. This is not what Abraham did. You are doing the works your father did."

→ Not pulling any punches. - PB

They said to him, "We were not born of sexual immorality. We have one Father— even God." Jesus said to them, "If God were your Father, you would love me, for I came from God and I am here. I came not of my own accord, but he sent me. Why do you not understand what I say? It is because you cannot bear to hear my word. You are of your father the devil, and your will is to do your father's desires. He was a murderer from the beginning, and has nothing to do with the truth, because there is no truth in him. When he lies, he speaks out of his own character, for he is a liar and the father of lies. But because I tell the truth, you do not believe me. Which one of you convicts me of sin? If I tell the truth, why do you not believe me? Whoever is of God hears the words of God. The reason why you do not hear them is that you are not of God."

Left hook to the jaw! - PB

Massive uppercut! - PB

Knockout! - PB

Before Abraham Was, I Am

The Jews answered him, "Are we not right in saying that you are a Samaritan and have a demon?"

Hey man don't you have a demon? Crazy. - D

Jesus answered, "I do not have a demon, but I honor my Father, and you dishonor me. Yet I do not seek my own glory; there is One who seeks it, and he is the judge. Truly, truly, I say to you, if anyone keeps my word, he will never see death."

The Jews said to him, "Now we know that you have a demon! Abraham died, as did the prophets, yet you say, "If anyone keeps my word, he will never taste death." Are you greater than our father Abraham, who died? And the prophets died! Who do you make yourself out to be?" *Calling him a poser. - PB*

Jesus answered, "If I glorify myself, my glory is nothing. It is my Father who glorifies me, of whom you say, 'He is our God.' But you have not known him. I know him. If I were to say that I do not know him, I would be a liar like you, but I do know him and I keep his word. Your father Abraham rejoiced that he would see my day. He saw it and was glad." *Back at it again! - PB*

So the Jews said to him, "You are not yet fifty years old, and have you seen Abraham?" Jesus said to them, "Truly, truly, I say to you, before Abraham was, I am." So they picked up stones to throw at him, but Jesus hid himself and went out of the temple. *My pastor said it's a big deal when Jesus says "I am" because that's how God talked about Himself in the Old Testament part of the Bible. For Jesus to claim to be the "I am" was like total blasphemy to the Jewish leaders. That's probably why they grabbed rocks to throw at him. - Tay*

CHAPTER 9

Jesus Heals a Man Born Blind

As he passed by, he saw a man blind from birth. And his disciples asked him, "Rabbi, who sinned, this man or his parents, that he was born blind?" Jesus answered, "It was not that this man sinned, or his parents, but that the works of God might be displayed in him. We must work the works of him who sent me while it is day; night is coming, when no one can work. As long as I am in the world, I am the light of the world."

A purpose for blindness? My sister is deaf, wonder what the purpose is for that? - PB

Having said these things, he spat on the ground and made mud with the saliva. Then he anointed the man's eyes with the mud and said to him, "Go, wash in the pool of Siloam" (which means Sent). So he went and washed and came back seeing.

The neighbors and those who had seen him before as a beggar were saying, "Is this not the man who used to sit and beg?" Some said, "It is he." Others said, "No, but he is like him." He kept saying, "I am the man." So they said to him, "Then how were your eyes opened?" He answered, "The man called Jesus made mud and anointed my eyes and said to me, 'Go to Siloam and wash.' So I went and washed and received my sight." They said to him, "Where is he?" He said, "I do not know."

They brought to the Pharisees the man who had formerly been blind. Now it was a Sabbath day when Jesus made the mud and opened his eyes. So the Pharisees again asked him how he had received his sight. And he said to them, "He put mud on my eyes, and I washed, and I see." Some of the Pharisees said, "This man is not from God, for he does not keep the Sabbath." But others said, "How can a man who is a sinner do such signs?" And there was a division among them.

So they said again to the blind man, "What do you say about him, since he has opened your eyes?" He said, "He is a prophet." The Jews did not believe that he had been blind and had received his sight, until they called the parents of the man who had received his sight and asked them, "Is this your son, who you say was born blind? How then does he now see?"

The Life Book   47

Handwritten annotations:

♡ Nasty! – V

Wonder why he used mud this time? – D

♡ can't imagine trying to get people to believe you – V

Shaking things up again – my kind of guy. – PB

I don't get these Pharisee people. He does something good again on the Sabbath and they don't like it. – D

His parents answered, "We know that this is our son and that he was born blind. But how he now sees we do not know, nor do we know who opened his eyes. Ask him; he is of age. He will speak for himself." (His parents said these things because they feared the Jews, for the Jews had already agreed that if anyone should confess Jesus to be Christ, he was to be put out of the synagogue.) Therefore his parents said, "He is of age; ask him."

So for the second time they called the man who had been blind and said to him, "Give glory to God. We know that this man is a sinner." He answered, "Whether he is a sinner I do not know. One thing I do know, that though I was blind, now I see."

They said to him, "What did he do to you? How did he open your eyes?" He answered them, "I have told you already, and you would not listen. Why do you want to hear it again? Do you also want to become his disciples?"

And they reviled him, saying, "You are his disciple, but we are disciples of Moses. We know that God has spoken to Moses, but as for this man, we do not know where he comes from." The man answered, "Why, this is an amazing thing! You do not know where he comes from, and yet he opened my eyes. We know that God does not listen to sinners, but if anyone is a worshiper of God and does his will, God listens to him. Never since the world began has it been heard that anyone opened the eyes of a man born blind. If this man were not from God, he could do nothing." They answered him, "You were born in utter sin, and would you teach us?" And they cast him out.

Jesus heard that they had cast him out, and having found him he said, "Do you believe in the Son of Man?" He answered, "And who is he, sir, that I may believe in him?" Jesus said to him, "You have seen him, and it is he who is speaking to you." He said, "Lord, I believe," and he worshiped him.

→ Tough to not believe when you were blind and now you're not. – PB

Jesus said, "For judgment I came into this world, that those who do not see may see, and those who see may become blind." Some of the Pharisees near him heard these things, and said to him, "Are we also blind?" Jesus said to them, "If you were blind, you would have no guilt; but now that you say, 'We see,' your guilt remains."

Sometimes he says confusing things that I have to really think about. – V

CHAPTER 10

Dad took me to a petting zoo once. I learned that sheep's wool feels strange and its not a good idea to try to head butt a goat. – D

I Am the Good Shepherd

"Truly, truly, I say to you, he who does not enter the sheepfold by the door but climbs in by another way, that man is a thief and a robber. But he who enters by the door is the shepherd of the sheep. To him the gatekeeper opens. The sheep hear his voice, and he calls his own sheep by name and leads them out. When he has brought out all his own, he goes before them, and the sheep follow him, for they know his voice. A stranger they will not follow, but they will flee from him, for they do not know the voice of strangers."

This figure of speech Jesus used with them, but they did not understand what he was saying to them.

Me either. – V

So Jesus again said to them, "Truly, truly, I say to you, I am the door of the sheep. All who came before me are thieves and robbers, but the sheep did not listen to them. I am the door. If anyone enters by me, he will be saved and will go in and out and find pasture. The thief comes only to steal and kill and destroy. I came that they may have life and have it <u>abundantly</u>. I am the good shepherd. The good shepherd lays down his life for the sheep. He who is a hired hand and not a shepherd, who does not own the sheep, sees the wolf coming and leaves the sheep and flees, and the wolf snatches them and scatters them. He flees because he is a hired hand and cares nothing for the sheep. I am the good shepherd. I know my own and my own know me, just as the Father knows me and I know the Father; and I lay down my life for the sheep.

I think a lot of people believe that if they decided to follow Jesus that life would be lame and boring. I like this part because Jesus is saying that the best life comes when you follow him. — Tay

Ah...foreshadowing. English class taught me something. — PB

"I am the good shepherd. I know my own and my own know me, just as the Father knows me and I know the Father; and I lay down my life for the sheep. And I have other sheep that are not of this fold. I must bring them also, and they will listen to my voice. So there will be one flock, one shepherd.

I hope I'm one of them — V

"For this reason the Father loves me, because I lay down my life that I may take it up again. No one takes it from me, but I lay it down of my own accord. I have authority to lay it down, and I have authority to take it up again. This charge I have received from my Father."

Guess he's saying that he could've avoided being killed, but he allowed himself to be killed for the sake of his sheep. That changes things for me. I thought they just took him and killed him. — D

There was again a division among the Jews because of these words. Many of them said, "He has a demon, and is insane; why listen to him?" Others said, "These are not the words of one who is oppressed by a demon. Can a demon open the eyes of the blind?"

↳ Split decision. — PB

I and the Father Are One

[handwritten: wonder if they get snow? - V ♡]

At that time the Feast of Dedication took place at Jerusalem. It was winter, and Jesus was walking in the temple, in the colonnade of Solomon. So the Jews gathered around him and said to him, "How long will you keep us in suspense? If you are the Christ, tell us plainly."

Jesus answered them, "I told you, and you do not believe. The works that I do in my Father's name bear witness about me, but you do not believe because you are not part of my flock. My sheep hear my voice, and I know them, and they follow me. I give them eternal life, and they will never perish, and no one will snatch them out of my hand. My Father, who has given them to me, is greater than all, and no one is able to snatch them out of the Father's hand. I and the Father are one.*"

*[handwritten: *He's saying He is one with God - that He is divine. That really seems to upset the Jews as being blasphemous. - Uncle G.]*

The Jews picked up stones again to stone him. Jesus answered them, "I have shown you many good works from the Father; for which of them are you going to stone me?"

[handwritten: → Good question. - PB]

The Jews answered him, "It is not for a good work that we are going to stone you but for blasphemy, because you, being a man, make yourself God." Jesus answered them, "Is it not written in your Law, 'I said, you are gods'? If he called them gods to whom the word of God came—and Scripture cannot be broken— do you say of him whom the Father consecrated and sent into the world, 'You are blaspheming,' because I said, 'I am the Son of God'? If I am not doing the works of my Father, then do not believe me; but if I do them, even though you do not believe me, believe the works, that you may know and understand that the

[handwritten: Take your pick. - D]

Father is in me and I am in the Father." Again they sought to arrest him, but he escaped from their hands.

He has great escapability. — PB

He went away again across the Jordan to the place where John had been baptizing at first, and there he remained. And many came to him. And they said, "John did no sign, but everything that John said about this man was true." And many believed in him there.

CHAPTER II

The Death of Lazarus

Now a certain man was ill, Lazarus of Bethany, the village of Mary and her sister Martha. It was Mary who anointed the Lord with ointment and wiped his feet with her hair, whose brother Lazarus was ill. So the sisters sent to him, saying, "Lord, he whom you love is ill."

That's kind of gross — V

But when Jesus heard it he said, "This illness does not lead to death. It is for the glory of God, so that the Son of God may be glorified through it."

Now Jesus loved Martha and her sister and Lazarus. So, when he heard that Lazarus was ill, he stayed two days longer in the place where he was. Then after this he said to the disciples, "Let us go to Judea again."

The disciples said to him, "Rabbi, the Jews were just now seeking to stone you, and are you going there again?"

They must think he's crazy. — D

The Life Book...Got Questions? Ask the person who gave you The Life Book .

Jesus answered, "Are there not twelve hours in the day? If anyone walks in the day, he does not stumble, because he sees the light of this world. But if anyone walks in the night, he stumbles, because the light is not in him."

Not sure what that has to do with getting stoned by the Jews???? - PB

After saying these things, he said to them, "Our friend Lazarus has fallen asleep, but I go to awaken him." The disciples said to him, "Lord, if he has fallen asleep, he will recover." Now Jesus had spoken of his death, but they thought that he meant taking rest in sleep.

Seems like you need a secret decoder ring sometimes to figure out what Jesus is saying,

Then Jesus told them plainly, "Lazarus has died, and for your sake I am glad *or maybe I'm just a* that I was not there, so that you may believe. But let us go to him." So Thomas, *geek. - D* called the Twin, said to his fellow disciples, "Let us also go, that we may die with him."

Uh yeah, I'll be right behind you. - D

I Am the Resurrection and the Life

Now when Jesus came, he found that Lazarus had already been in the tomb four days. Bethany was near Jerusalem, about two miles off, and many of the Jews had come to Martha and Mary to console them concerning their brother. So when Martha heard that Jesus was coming, she went and met him, but Mary remained seated in the house. Martha said to Jesus, "Lord, if you had been here, my brother would not have died. But even now I know that whatever you ask from God, God will give you."

Jesus said to her, "Your brother will rise again." Martha said to him, "I know that he will rise again in the resurrection on the last day." Jesus said to her, "I am the resurrection and the life. Whoever believes in me, though he die, yet shall he live. Everyone who lives and believes in Me will never die—ever. Do you believe this?"

Heard this at Easter. - V

Believe, believe, believe. Wonder how many times Jesus says "Believe"? - PB

She said to him, "Yes, Lord; I believe that you are the Christ, the Son of God, who is coming into the world."

Jesus Weeps

When she had said this, she went and called her sister Mary, saying in private, "The Teacher is here and is calling for you." And when she heard it, she rose quickly and went to him. Now Jesus had not yet come into the village, but was still in the place where Martha had met him. When the Jews who were with her in the house, consoling her, saw Mary rise quickly and go out, they followed her, supposing that she was going to the tomb to weep there. Now when Mary came to where Jesus was and saw him, she fell at his feet, saying to him, "Lord, if you had been here, my brother would not have died."

She had some real faith. — Tay

When Jesus saw her weeping, and the Jews who had come with her also weeping, he was deeply moved in his spirit and greatly troubled. And he said, "Where have you laid him?" They said to him, "Lord, come and see." Jesus wept. So the Jews said, "See how he loved him!" But some of them said, "Could not he who opened the eyes of the blind man also have kept this man from dying?"

Jesus cries? This is probably the coolest part for me so far. Nice to know that even though He's perfect and divine that he still cries when he sees people he loves crying. — V

Jesus Raises Lazarus

Then Jesus, deeply moved again, came to the tomb. It was a cave, and a stone lay against it. Jesus said, "Take away the stone." Martha, the sister of the dead man, said to him, "Lord, by this time there will be an odor, for he has been dead four days."

New cologne - Ode to Dead Body. Nasty. — PB

Jesus said to her, "Did I not tell you that if you believed you would see the glory of God?" So they took away the stone.

And Jesus lifted up his eyes and said, "Father, I thank you that you have heard me. I knew that you always hear me, but I said this on account of the people standing around, that they may believe that you sent me." When he had said these things, he cried out with a loud voice, "Lazarus, come out." The man who had died came out, his hands and feet bound with linen strips, and his face wrapped with a cloth. Jesus said to them, "Unbind him, and let him go."

How is this even possible? The guy was dead for four days! Seriously, if I saw this happen, that would be proof enough for me that he was who he said he was - D

The Plot to Kill Jesus

Many of the Jews therefore, who had come with Mary and had seen what he did, believed in him, but some of them went to the Pharisees and told them what Jesus had done. So the chief priests and the Pharisees gathered the Council and said, "What are we to do? For this man performs many signs. If we let him go on like this, everyone will believe in him, and the Romans will come and take away both our place and our nation."

This is hilarious! "Oh no, he's doing too much good stuff and everyone will like him! We have to take him out now!" Are you kidding me?- PB

But one of them, Caiaphas, who was high priest that year, said to them, "You know nothing at all. Nor do you understand that it is better for you that one man should die for the people, not that the whole nation should perish." He did not say this of his own accord, but being high priest that year he prophesied that Jesus would die for the nation, and not for the nation only, but also to gather into one the children of God who are scattered abroad. So from that day on they made plans to put him to death.

He got that prophecy right! - Tay

Religious leaders become Hit Men. I used to think Jesus was a nice guy who brought peace and love. Looks more like people either loved him or hated him. - D

Jesus therefore no longer walked openly among the Jews, but went from there to the region near the wilderness, to a town called Ephraim, and there he stayed with the disciples. Now the Passover of the Jews was at hand, and many went up from the country to Jerusalem before the Passover to purify themselves. They were looking for Jesus and saying to one another as they stood in the temple, "What do you think? That he will not come to the feast at all?" Now the chief priests and the Pharisees had given orders that if anyone knew where he was, he should let them know, so that they might arrest him.

CHAPTER 12

Mary Anoints Jesus at Bethany

Six days before the Passover, Jesus therefore came to Bethany, where Lazarus was, whom Jesus had raised from the dead. So they gave a dinner for him there. Martha served, and Lazarus was one of those reclining with him at table. Mary therefore took a pound of expensive ointment made from pure nard, and anointed the feet of Jesus and wiped his feet with her hair. The house was filled with the fragrance of the perfume. But Judas Iscariot, one of his disciples (he who was about to betray him), said, "Why was this ointment not sold for three hundred denarii and given to the poor?" He said this, not because he cared about the poor, but because he was a thief, and having charge of the moneybag he used to help himself to what was put into it. Jesus said, "Leave her alone, so that she may keep it for the day of my burial. For the poor you always have with you, but you do not always have me."

Has his mind on the money and the money on his mind. – PB

It must be weird to know: 1. You're going to be killed even though you're innocent of any crime 2. It's going to hurt big time 3. The people you're dying for are the ones who want to kill you – PB

The Plot to Kill Lazarus

When the large crowd of the Jews learned that Jesus was there, they came, not only on account of him but also to see Lazarus, whom he had raised from the dead. So the chief priests made plans to put Lazarus to death as well, because on account of him many of the Jews were going away and believing in Jesus.

Seriously wicked priests! - D

The Triumphal Entry

The next day the large crowd that had come to the feast heard that Jesus was coming to Jerusalem. So they took branches of palm trees and went out to meet him, crying out, "Hosanna! Blessed is he who comes in the name of the Lord, even the King of Israel!" And Jesus found a young donkey and sat on it, just as it is written, "Fear not, daughter of Zion; behold, your king is coming, sitting on a donkey's colt!"

So much for flying under the radar when people are looking to kill you. - PB

His disciples did not understand these things at first, but when Jesus was glorified, then they remembered that these things had been written about him and had been done to him. The crowd that had been with him when he called Lazarus out of the tomb and raised him from the dead continued to bear witness. The reason why the crowd went to meet him was that they heard he had done this sign. So the Pharisees said to one another, "You see that you are gaining nothing. Look, the world has gone after him."

Jealous? - V

Some Greeks Seek Jesus

Now among those who went up to worship at the feast were some Greeks. So these came to Philip, who was from Bethsaida in Galilee, and asked him, "Sir, we wish to see Jesus." Philip went and told Andrew; Andrew and Philip went and told Jesus.

And Jesus answered them, "The hour has come for the Son of Man to be glorified. Truly, truly, I say to you, unless a grain of wheat falls into the earth and dies, it remains alone; but if it dies, it bears much fruit. Whoever loves his life loses it, and whoever hates his life in this world will keep it for (eternal life.)

Hmmm. Have to think about that one. - D

"If anyone serves me, he must follow me; and where I am, there will my servant be also. If anyone serves me, the Father will honor him.

The Son of Man Must Be Lifted Up
"Now is my soul troubled. And what shall I say? 'Father, save me from this hour'? But for this purpose I have come to this hour. Father, glorify your name."

♡ WOW! - V

Then a voice came from heaven: "I have glorified it, and I will glorify it again." The crowd that stood there and heard it said that it had thundered. Others said, "An angel has spoken to him." Jesus answered, "This voice has come for your sake, not mine. Now is the judgment of this world; now will the ruler of this world be cast out. And I, when I am lifted up from the earth, will draw all people to myself."

It would work on me. - V

He said this to show by what kind of death he was going to die. So the crowd answered him, "We have heard from the Law that the Christ remains forever. How can you say that the Son of Man must be lifted up? Who is this Son of Man?" So Jesus said to them, "The light is among you for a little while longer. Walk while you have the light, lest darkness overtake you. The one who walks in the darkness does not know where he is going. While you have the light, believe in the light, that you may become sons of light."

He never seems to directly answer any questions. I actually kind of like that about him. He does his own thing. - PB

The Unbelief of the People

When Jesus had said these things, he departed and hid himself from them. Though he had done so many signs before them, they still did not believe in him, so that the word spoken by the prophet Isaiah might be fulfilled: "Lord, who has believed what he heard from us, and to whom has the arm of the Lord been revealed?" Therefore they could not believe. For again Isaiah said, "He has <u>blinded their eyes and hardened their heart</u>, lest they see with their eyes, and understand with their heart, and turn, and I would heal them." Isaiah said these things because he saw his glory and spoke of him.

It's hard to think about God blinding their eyes and hardening their hearts. I wish he'd soften my dad's heart. — Tay

Nevertheless, many even of the authorities believed in him, but for fear of the Pharisees they did not <u>confess it</u>, so that they would not be put out of the synagogue; for they loved the glory that comes from man more than the glory that comes from God.

That's me too. But I guess I'm just starting to understand what Jesus and God is all about as I go through this. So maybe things will change. —V

Jesus Came to Save the World

And Jesus cried out and said, "Whoever believes in me, believes not in me but in him who sent me. And whoever sees me sees him who sent me. I have come into the world as light, so that whoever believes in me may not remain in darkness.

"If anyone hears my words and does not keep them, I do not judge him; for I did not come to judge the world but to save the world. The one who rejects me and does not receive my words has a judge; the word that I have spoken will judge

How could they not believe in him after seeing everything he'd done? —V

Can you be a secret believer in Jesus? — Tay.

him on the last day. For I have not spoken on my own authority, but the Father who sent me has himself given me a commandment—what to say and what to speak. And I know that his commandment is eternal life. What I say, therefore, I say as the Father has told me."

You reject me? Deal with my dad!
- PB

CHAPTER 13

Jesus Washes the Disciples' Feet

Now before the Feast of the Passover, when Jesus knew that his hour had come to depart out of this world to the Father, having loved his own who were in the world, he loved them to the end.

Freaky to think the devil puts stuff in our hearts. - V

During supper, when the devil had already put it into the heart of Judas Iscariot, Simon's son, to betray him, Jesus, knowing that the Father had given all things into his hands, and that he had come from God and was going back to God, rose from supper. He laid aside his outer garments, and taking a towel, tied it around his waist. Then he poured water into a basin and began to wash the disciples' feet and to wipe them with the towel that was wrapped around him.

Feet are nasty! - Tay

He came to Simon Peter, who said to him, "Lord, do you wash my feet?" Jesus answered him, "What I am doing you do not understand now, but afterward you will understand." Peter said to him, "You shall never wash my feet." Jesus answered him, "If I do not wash you, you have no share with me."

What's with the foot washing thing? Seems like a weird thing to do. - D

*When my momma was near the end, I had to do everything for her. Give her baths, cook her food, change her diapers, brush her hair and teeth...everything. It was the most humbling experience of my life. I learned a lot about being a servant. She did all that for me when I was a baby. I think washing feet is like that. Feet back then were nasty because it was dirty and dusty. They probably smelled terrible and were caked with dirt and grime. For the son of God to wash his follower's feet would have been upside down. This shows Jesus being willing to not only die for us, but to stoop to the lowest level to serve us. Amazing!

- Uncle G.

Simon Peter said to him, "Lord, not my feet only but also my hands and my head!" Jesus said to him, "The one who has bathed does not need to wash, except for his feet, but is completely clean. And you are clean, but not every one of you." For he knew who was to betray him; that was why he said, "Not all of you are clean."

All or nothing. Lord, wash all of me. — Tay

When he had washed their feet and put on his outer garments and resumed his place, he said to them, "Do you understand what I have done to you? You call me Teacher and Lord, and you are right, for so I am. If I then, your Lord and Teacher, have washed your feet, you also ought to wash one another's feet. For I have given you an example, that you also should do just as I have done to you.

Do Christians do this anymore? — D

"Truly, truly, I say to you, a servant is not greater than his master, nor is a messenger greater than the one who sent him. If you know these things, blessed are you if you do them. I am not speaking of all of you; I know whom I have chosen. But the Scripture will be fulfilled, 'He who ate my bread has lifted his heel against me.'

Wonder if he winked at Judas when he said this. — PB

"I am telling you this now, before it takes place, that when it does take place you may believe that I am he. Truly, truly, I say to you, whoever receives the one I send receives me, and whoever receives me receives the one who sent me."

One of You Will Betray Me

♡ No doubt. — V

After saying these things, Jesus was troubled in his spirit, and testified, "Truly, truly, I say to you, one of you will betray me."

The disciples looked at one another, uncertain of whom he spoke. One of his disciples, whom Jesus loved, was reclining at table close to Jesus, so Simon Peter motioned to him to ask Jesus of whom he was speaking. So that disciple, leaning back against Jesus, said to him, "Lord, who is it?"

I think this Peter guy wanted to crush the traitor before he did the deed. - D

Jesus answered, "It is he to whom I will give this morsel of bread when I have dipped it." So when he had dipped the morsel, he gave it to Judas, the son of Simon Iscariot. Then after he had taken the morsel, Satan entered into him.

I don't want to know what that feels like. I wonder if you could tell just by looking at him. Scary. - V

Jesus said to him, "What you are going to do, do quickly." Now no one at the table knew why he said this to him. Some thought that, because Judas had the moneybag, Jesus was telling him, "Buy what we need for the feast," or that he should give something to the poor. So, after receiving the morsel of bread, he immediately went out. And it was night.

Surprised Peter didn't jump across the table and pound him right away. - PB

A New Commandment

When he had gone out, Jesus said, "Now is the Son of Man glorified, and God is glorified in him. If God is glorified in him, God will also glorify him in himself, and glorify him at once. Little children, yet a little while I am with you. You will seek me, and just as I said to the Jews, so now I also say to you, "Where I am going you cannot come.

"A new commandment I give to you, that you love one another: just as I have loved you, you also are to love one another. By this all people will know that you are my disciples, if you have love for one another."

I've seen a lot of people who call themselves Christians that don't seem to love anybody but themselves. - D

Jesus Foretells Peter's Denial

Simon Peter said to him, "Lord, where are you going?" Jesus answered him, "Where I am going you cannot follow me now, but you will follow afterward." Peter said to him, "Lord, why can I not follow you now? I will lay down my life for you." Jesus answered, "Will you lay down your life for me? Truly, truly, I say to you, the rooster will not crow till you have denied me three times."

I hope I would've said the same thing. — Tay

CHAPTER 14

I Am the Way, and the Truth, and the Life

"Let not your hearts be troubled. Believe in God; believe also in me. In my Father's house are many rooms; if it were not so, I would have told you; for I go to prepare a place for you. And if I go and prepare a place for you, I will come again and will take you to myself, that where I am you may be also. And you know the way to where I am going."

I can't wait until I see the place he prepared for me! — Tay

Thomas said to him, "Lord, we do not know where you are going. How can we know the way?" Jesus said to him, "I am the way, and the truth, and the life. No one comes to the Father except through me.

Heard this one before. Guess if he says he's the truth then anything that doesn't agree with him is false, right? Big claim, but if he is who he says he is I guess he can say he's the truth - D

If you had known me, you would have known my Father also. From now on you do know him and have seen him." Philip said to him, "Lord, show us the Father, and it is enough for us."

Jesus said to him, "Have I been with you so long, and you still do not know me, Philip? Whoever has seen me has seen the Father. How can you say, 'Show us the Father'? Do you not believe that I am in the Father and the Father is in me? The words that I say to you I do not speak on my own authority, but the Father who dwells in me does his works. Believe me that I am in the Father and the Father is in me, or else believe on account of the works themselves.

See my note on the next page.

Kind of weird the whole idea of them being united. – V

"Truly, truly, I say to you, whoever believes in me will also do the works that I do; and greater works than these will he do, because I am going to the Father. Whatever you ask in my name, this I will do, that the Father may be glorified in the Son. If you ask me anything in my name, I will do it.

Whoa! Never heard that one. – PB

I think he's talking about doing things for us that honor God. – Tay

Jesus Promises the Holy Spirit

"If you love me, you will keep my commandments. And I will ask the Father, and he will give you another Helper, to be with you forever, even the Spirit of truth, whom the world cannot receive, because it neither sees him nor knows him. You know him, for he dwells with you and will be in you.

Never heard this before. Jesus is taking off, but sending some kind of spirit to take his place. A little weird because I don't think you can see a spirit, but cool that he's not just ditching his followers. – D

"I will not leave you as orphans; I will come to you. Yet a little while and the world will see me no more, but you will see me. Because I live, you also will live. In that day you will know that I am in my Father, and you in me, and I in you. Whoever has my commandments and keeps them, he it is who loves me. And he who loves me will be loved by my Father, and I will love him and manifest myself to him."

He's into this whole me and the Father are one thing. Keeps saying it over and over. – D

Hey V, this is the whole trinity thing. God the Father, God the Son and God the Holy Spirit are all one. One God in three persons. I know it's hard to understand, but we aren't God and there are some things we will not be able to grasp. There is a verse in the Bible that says, who can understand the mind of God? And another verse that says, His ways are higher than our ways and His thoughts higher than our thoughts. I don't really fully understand the trinity either, but I believe it. I don't understand love, but I believe in it. I don't understand flight, but I see planes flying. Jesus is one with the Father.

- Uncle G.

Judas (not Iscariot) said to him, "Lord, how is it that you will manifest yourself to us, and not to the world?" Jesus answered him, "If anyone loves me, he will keep my word, and my Father will love him, and we will come to him and make our home with him. Whoever does not love me does not keep my words. And the word that you hear is not mine but the Father's who sent me. "These things I have spoken to you while I am still with you. But the Helper, the Holy Spirit, whom the Father will send in my name, he will teach you all things and bring to your remembrance all that I have said to you.* See my note on the next page.

How's that work? - PB

"Peace I leave with you; my peace I give to you. Not as the world gives do I give to you. Let not your hearts be troubled, neither let them be afraid. You heard me say to you, "I am going away, and I will come to you." If you loved me, you would have rejoiced, because I am going to the Father, for the Father is greater than I. And now I have told you before it takes place, so that when it does take place you may believe. ——> Pretty sure I'd believe if someone told me what was going to happen and it did. - PB

"I will no longer talk much with you, for the ruler of this world is coming. He has no claim on me, but I do as the Father has commanded me, so that the world may know that I love the Father. Rise, let us go from here.

CHAPTER 15

I Am the True Vine

"I am the true vine, and my Father is the vinedresser. Every branch in me that does not bear fruit he takes away, and every branch that does bear fruit he prunes, that it may bear more fruit. Already you are clean because of the word that I have spoken to you.

Apples? Oranges? Pears? - PB

*I remember one winter when I was about 8, Sheila (the neighbor girl) and I were at the little market on the corner. Her mom had given her 25 cents for candy. She wanted a big bag of hard candies so we could share, but it was 50 cents. Without thinking much about it, I grabbed the bag and shoved it inside my coat. As soon as I started to leave, I heard my mom's voice playing in my head. "Gideon Ronald Williams II, you make sure and represent that name with honor to make your Grandpa proud." Blood rushed to my head along with a heaping portion of guilt and I put the candy bag back on the shelf I think that's how the Holy Spirit works in the lives of believers in Jesus. God puts the Holy Spirit inside of you when you decide to accept His forgiveness and believe in Jesus. Then the Holy Spirit kind of nudges, guides and directs you to do what pleases God - kind of like momma's voice in my head.

- Uncle G.

So, if Fruit is the good stuff for God and people, then that's what proves a person is a believer in Jesus? If that's true, then believing in Jesus seems to be a bit more than just saying you believe - you must have to really believe in a way that changes your life. I like that much better than just saying, "Yeah, okay, sure I believe" and then nothing changes. Not sure I'm ready to go there yet, but I'd rather something like this totally change everything about me, than just be something I say. - D

68 The Life Book...Got Questions? Ask the person who gave you The Life Book

"Abide in me, and I in you. As the branch cannot bear fruit by itself, unless it abides in the vine, neither can you, unless you abide in me.

I think the fruit is the good stuff we do for God and others — like helping them come to believe in Jesus and showing them love when no one else loves them — stuff like that.
— Tay

"I am the vine; you are the branches. Whoever abides in me and I in him, he it is that bears much fruit, for apart from me you can do nothing. If anyone does not abide in me he is thrown away like a branch and withers; and the branches are gathered, thrown into the fire, and burned. If you abide in me, and my words abide in you, ask whatever you wish, and it will be done for you. By this my Father is glorified, that you bear much fruit and so prove to be my disciples.

I want to stay attached to the vine.
— Tay

"As the Father has loved me, so have I loved you. Abide in my love. If you keep my commandments, you will abide in my love, just as I have kept my Father's commandments and abide in his love. These things I have spoken to you, that my joy may be in you, and that your joy may be full.

Having more joy in my life would be good. Most of the time I have the opposite. — V

"This is my commandment, that you love one another as I have loved you. Greater love has no one than this, that someone lay down his life for his friends. You are my friends if you do what I command you. No longer do I call you servants, for the servant does not know what his master is doing; but I have called you friends, for all that I have heard from my Father I have made known to you. *AWESOME! Jesus is not just my savior and the son of God — he's also my friend. — Tay*

"You did not choose me, but I chose you and appointed you that you should go and bear fruit and that your fruit should abide, so that whatever you ask the Father in my name, he may give it to you. These things I command you, so that you will love one another. *Different definition of love than I'm used to. I've told my girl I love her, but not sure I'd die for her. (Hope she doesn't read this!) — PB*

The Hatred of the World

"If the world hates you, know that it has hated me before it hated you. If you were of the world, the world would love you as its own; but because you are not of the world, but I chose you out of the world, therefore (the world hates you)

I can see the commercial now - "Follow Jesus and be hated". - D

"Remember the word that I said to you: 'A servant is not greater than his master.' If they persecuted me, they will also persecute you. If they kept my word, they will also keep yours. But all these things they will do to you on account of my name, because they do not know him who sent me.

"If I had not come and spoken to them, they would not have been guilty of sin, but now they have no excuse for their sin. Whoever hates me hates my Father also. If I had not done among them the works that no one else did, they would not be guilty of sin, but now they have seen and hated both me and my Father. But the word that is written in their Law must be fulfilled: 'They hated me without a cause.' *My younger brother is great at excuses and they always work to get him out of trouble. Yeah. I'm a bit jealous. - V*

"But when the Helper comes, whom I will send to you from the Father, the Spirit of truth, who proceeds from the Father, he will bear witness about me. And you also will bear witness, because you have been with me from the beginning.

CHAPTER 16

Can't imagine that happening today - banned from church. Probably wouldn't go over very well. - PB

"I have said all these things to you to keep you from falling away. They will put you out of the synagogues. Indeed, the hour is coming when whoever kills you will think he is offering service to God. And they will do these things because they have not known the Father, nor me. But I have said these things to you, that when their hour comes you may remember that I told them to you.

The Work of the Holy Spirit

"I did not say these things to you from the beginning, because I was with you. But now I am going to him who sent me, and none of you asks me, 'Where are you going?' But because I have said these things to you, sorrow has filled your heart. Nevertheless, I tell you the truth: it is to your advantage that I go away, for if I do not go away, the Helper will not come to you. But if I go, I will send him to you.

I'd be bummed too if I left everything to follow him and now he's taking off. — D

"And when he comes, he will convict the world concerning sin and righteousness and judgment: concerning sin, because they do not believe in me; concerning righteousness, because I go to the Father, and you will see me no longer; concerning judgment, because the ruler of this world is judged. I still have many things to say to you, but you cannot bear them now.

Job #2 of Holy Spirit: Make sure everyone knows they're on the hook for their sin? — PB

"When the Spirit of truth comes, he will guide you into all the truth, for he will not speak on his own authority, but whatever he hears he will speak, and he will declare to you the things that are to come. He will glorify me, for he will take what is mine and declare it to you. All that the Father has is mine; therefore I said that he will take what is mine and declare it to you.

Your Sorrow Will Turn into Joy

"A little while, and you will see me no longer; and again a little while, and you will see me." So some of his disciples said to one another, "What is this that he

I'm confused too. — V

says to us, 'A little while, and you will not see me, and again a little while, and you will see me'; and, 'because I am going to the Father'?"

So they were saying, "What does he mean by 'a little while'? We do not know what he is talking about."

Jesus knew that they wanted to ask him, so he said to them, "Is this what you are asking yourselves, what I meant by saying, 'A little while and you will not see me, and again a little while and you will see me'? Truly, truly, I say to you, you will weep and lament, but the <u>world will rejoice.</u> You will be sorrowful, but your sorrow will turn into joy.

I think he's talking about when he is murdered on the cross. — Tay

"When a woman is giving birth, she has sorrow because her hour has come, but when she has delivered the baby, she no longer remembers the anguish, for joy that a human being has been born into the world. So also you have sorrow now, but I will see you again, and your hearts will rejoice, and no one will take your joy from you.

"In that day you will ask nothing of me. Truly, truly, I say to you, whatever you ask of the Father in my name, he will give it to you. Until now you have asked nothing in my name. Ask, and you will receive, that your joy may be full.

I Have Overcome the World
"I have said these things to you in figures of speech. The hour is coming when I will no longer speak to you in figures of speech but will tell you plainly about the Father. In that day you will ask in my name, and I do not say to you that I

will ask the Father on your behalf; for the Father himself loves you, because you have loved me and have believed that I came from God. I came from the Father and have come into the world, and now I am leaving the world and going to the Father."

→ Repeats this thing a lot. – PB

His disciples said, "Ah, now you are speaking plainly and not using figurative speech! Now we know that you know all things and do not need anyone to question you; this is why we believe that you came from God."

Jesus answered them, "Do you now believe? Behold, the hour is coming, indeed it has come, when you will be scattered, each to his own home, and will leave me alone. Yet I am not alone, for the Father is with me. I have said these things to you, that in me you may have peace. In the world you will have tribulation. But take heart; I have overcome the world."

I think he's talking about when they run and hide after Jesus gets arrested. – Tay

CHAPTER 17

Jesus Prays to His Father

When Jesus had spoken these words, he lifted up his eyes to heaven, and said, "Father, the hour has come; glorify your Son that the Son may glorify you, since you have given him authority over all flesh, to give eternal life to all whom you have given him.

"And this is eternal life, that they know you the only true God, and Jesus Christ whom you have sent.

→ Never thought of knowing God and Jesus Christ, as eternal life. In fact, didn't think much at all about knowing God before reading this and making comments. – PB

"I glorified you on earth, having accomplished the work that you gave me to do. And now, Father, glorify me in your own presence with the glory that I had with you before the world existed.

Jesus Prays for His Disciples

"I have manifested your name to the people whom you gave me out of the world. Yours they were, and you gave them to me, and they have kept your word. Now they know that everything that you have given me is from you. For I have given them the words that you gave me, and they have received them and have come to know in truth that I came from you; and they have believed that you sent me.

"I am praying for them. I am not praying for the world but for those whom you have given me, for they are yours. All mine are yours, and yours are mine, and I am glorified in them. And I am no longer in the world, but they are in the world, and I am coming to you. Holy Father, keep them in your name, which you have given me, that they may be one, even as we are one. While I was with them, I kept them in your name, which you have given me. I have guarded them, and not one of them has been lost except the son of destruction, that the Scripture might be fulfilled.

"But now I am coming to you, and these things I speak in the world, that they may have my joy fulfilled in themselves. I have given them your word, and the world has hated them because they are not of the world, just as I am not of the world. I do not ask that you take them out of the world, but that you keep them from the evil one. They are not of the world, just as I am not of the world.

I think it's great that Jesus prays for his followers. – V

Guessing the evil one is the devil. Not sure I want to follow Jesus yet, but I definitely don't want the devil messing with me. – D

"Sanctify them in the truth; your word is truth. As you sent me into the world, so I have sent them into the world. And for their sake I consecrate myself, that they also may be sanctified in truth.

"I do not ask for these only, but also for those who will believe in me through their word, that they may all be one, just as you, Father, are in me, and I in you, that they also may be in us, so that the world may believe that you have sent me. The glory that you have given me I have given to them, that they may be one even as we are one, I in them and you in me, that they may become perfectly one, so that the world may know that you sent me and loved them even as you loved me.

Keeps talking about the whole being ONE thing. Over and over and over. - PB

"Father, I desire that they also, whom you have given me, may be with me where I am, to see my glory that you have given me because you loved me before the foundation of the world. O righteous Father, even though the world does not know you, I know you, and these know that you have sent me. I made known to them your name, and I will continue to make it known, that the love with which you have loved me may be in them, and I in them."

Hey Vanessa, in another part of the Bible it says that Jesus is now sitting by God the Father and praying for his followers all the time. So if you decide to become a believer in Jesus, you can be sure he'll be talking to God the Father about you all the time. That's an amazing thing when you think about it.

- Uncle G.

CHAPTER 18

Betrayal and Arrest of Jesus

When Jesus had spoken these words, he went out with his disciples across the Kidron Valley, where there was a garden, which he and his disciples entered. Now Judas, who betrayed him, also knew the place, for Jesus often met there with his disciples. So Judas, having procured a band of soldiers and some officers from the chief priests and the Pharisees, went there with lanterns and torches and weapons.

Who needs enemies when you have friends like Judas - the ultimate frienemy? - V

Then Jesus, knowing all that would happen to him, came forward and said to them, "Whom do you seek?" They answered him, "Jesus of Nazareth." Jesus said to them, "I am he." Judas, who betrayed him, was standing with them.

→ Escaped every other time. - PB

When Jesus said to them, "I am he," they drew back and <u>fell to the ground.</u>

Were they afraid???? - Tay

So he asked them again, "Whom do you seek?" And they said, "Jesus of Nazareth." Jesus answered, "I told you that I am he. So, if you seek me, let these men go." This was to fulfill the word that he had spoken: "Of those whom you gave me I have lost not one."

→ OUCH! Peter goes crazy! - PB

Then Simon Peter, having a sword, drew it and struck the high priest's servant and cut off his right ear. (The servant's name was Malchus.) So Jesus said to Peter, "Put your sword into its sheath; shall I not drink the <u>cup</u> that the Father has given me?"

I'm not sure why he calls it a cup, but he's talking about suffering and dying - paying the price for our sin to make us right with God. - Tay

Jesus Faces Annas and Caiaphas

So the band of soldiers and their captain and the officers of the Jews arrested Jesus and bound him. First they led him to Annas, for he was the father-in-law of Caiaphas, who was high priest that year. It was Caiaphas who had advised the Jews that it would be expedient that one man should die for the people.

Peter Denies Jesus

Simon Peter followed Jesus, and so did another disciple. Since that disciple was known to the high priest, he entered with Jesus into the court of the high priest, but Peter stood outside at the door. So the other disciple, who was known to the high priest, went out and spoke to the servant girl who kept watch at the door, and brought Peter in.

The servant girl at the door said to Peter, "You also are not one of this man's disciples, are you?" He said, "I am not." Now the servants and officers had made a charcoal fire, because it was cold, and they were standing and warming themselves. Peter also was with them, standing and warming himself.

#1 Denial – Didn't Peter say earlier that he'd die for Jesus? I've had a few friends ditch me too. Not fun. – D

The High Priest Questions Jesus

The high priest then questioned Jesus about his disciples and his teaching. Jesus answered him, "I have spoken openly to the world. I have always taught in synagogues and in the temple, where all Jews come together. I have said nothing in secret. Why do you ask me? Ask those who have heard me what I said to them; they know what I said."

When he had said these things, one of the officers standing by struck Jesus with his hand, saying, "Is that how you answer the high priest?" Jesus answered him, "If what I said is wrong, bear witness about the wrong; but if what I said is right, why do you strike me?" Annas then sent him bound to Caiaphas the high priest.

Really? They slapped him! Weird. - PB

Guess he didn't know what to say. - D

Peter Denies Jesus Again

#2 Denial - D

Now Simon Peter was standing and warming himself. So they said to him, "You also are not one of his disciples, are you?" He denied it and said, "I am not." One of the servants of the high priest, a relative of the man whose ear Peter had cut off, asked, "Did I not see you in the garden with him?" Peter again denied it, and at once a rooster crowed.

#3 Denial - BAM Jesus nailed it. - D

Jesus Before Pilate

Then they led Jesus from the house of Caiaphas to the governor's headquarters. It was early morning. They themselves did not enter the governor's headquarters, so that they would not be defiled, but could eat the Passover. So Pilate went outside to them and said, "What accusation do you bring against this man?" They answered him, "If this man were not doing evil, we would not have delivered him over to you."

Can you please kill him for us? Nice guys. - D

Pilate said to them, "Take him yourselves and judge him by your own law." The Jews said to him, "It is not lawful for us to put anyone to death." This was to fulfill the word that Jesus had spoken to show by what kind of death he was going to die.

My Kingdom Is Not of This World

So Pilate entered his headquarters again and called Jesus and said to him, "Are you the King of the Jews?" Jesus answered, "Do you say this of your own accord, or did others say it to you about me?"

Pilate answered, "Am I a Jew? Your own nation and the chief priests have delivered you over to me. What have you done?"

Jesus answered, "My kingdom is not of this world. If my kingdom were of this world, my servants would have been fighting, that I might not be delivered over to the Jews. But my kingdom is not from the world."

So is Jesus against fighting? – V

Then Pilate said to him, "So you are a king?" Jesus answered, "You say that I am a king. For this purpose I was born and for this purpose I have come into the world—to bear witness to the truth. Everyone who is of the truth listens to my voice."

I think this is the hardest part for my dad believing that Jesus is THE truth and not just one out of a whole bunch of religions that are true. I'm still praying for him.
– Tay

Pilate said to him, "What is truth?"

After he had said this, he went back outside to the Jews and told them, "I find no guilt in him. But you have a custom that I should release one man for you at the Passover. So do you want me to release to you the King of the Jews?" They cried out again, "Not this man, but Barabbas!" Now Barabbas was a robber.

Pilate doesn't seem to want to kill him. – D

Sure seems like the people want him dead! Quick change from cheering him to killing him. Remind me never to be popular like that. – PB

CHAPTER 19

Jesus Delivered to Be Crucified

Goes from letting him off to pounding on him. – PB

Then Pilate took Jesus and flogged him. And the soldiers twisted together a crown of thorns and put it on his head and arrayed him in a purple robe. They came up to him, saying, "Hail, King of the Jews!" and struck him with their hands.

Pilate went out again and said to them, "See, I am bringing him out to you that you may know that I find no guilt in him."

okay, so he has him beaten and then says he's done nothing wrong. What kind of justice is that? – V

So Jesus came out, wearing the crown of thorns and the purple robe. Pilate said to them, "Behold the man!" When the chief priests and the officers saw him, they cried out, "Crucify him, crucify him!"

Pilate said to them, "Take him yourselves and crucify him, for I find no guilt in him."

Still trying to get off easy. – PB

That's strange. Why would such a powerful guy be afraid, unless he thought it might be true? – D

The Jews answered him, "We have a law, and according to that law he ought to die because he has made himself the Son of God." When Pilate heard this statement, he was even more afraid. He entered his headquarters again and said to Jesus, "Where are you from?" But Jesus gave him no answer.

So Pilate said to him, "You will not speak to me? Do you not know that I have authority to release you and authority to crucify you?"

Hey man! You should be begging me for your life! – PB

Jesus answered him, "You would have no authority over me at all unless it had been given you from above. Therefore he who delivered me over to you has the greater sin."

Jesus is the King of all Kings! – Tay

From then on Pilate sought to release him, but the Jews cried out, "If you release this man, you are not Caesar's friend. Everyone who makes himself a king opposes Caesar."

So when Pilate heard these words, he brought Jesus out and sat down on the judgment seat at a place called The Stone Pavement, and in Aramaic Gabbatha. Now it was the day of Preparation of the Passover. It was about the sixth hour. He said to the Jews, "Behold your King!" They cried out, "Away with him, away with him, crucify him!"

I didn't know Pilate tried so hard not to kill Jesus. - V

Pilate said to them, "Shall I crucify your King?" The chief priests answered, "We have no king but Caesar." So he delivered him over to them to be crucified.

Wonder how heavy that thing was? - PB

The Crucifixion

So they took Jesus, and he went out, bearing his own cross, to the place called The Place of a Skull, which in Aramaic is called Golgotha. There they crucified him, and with him two others, one on either side, and Jesus between them. Pilate also wrote an inscription and put it on the cross. It read, "Jesus of Nazareth, the King of the Jews."

Many of the Jews read this inscription, for the place where Jesus was crucified was near the city, and it was written in Aramaic, in Latin, and in Greek. So the chief priests of the Jews said to Pilate, "Do not write, 'The King of the Jews,' but rather, 'This man said, I am King of the Jews.'"

Pilate answered, "What I have written I have written."

I'm thinking Pilate believed Jesus was at least someone special. - D

When the soldiers had crucified Jesus, they took his garments and divided them into four parts, one part for each soldier; also his tunic.

But the tunic was seamless, woven in one piece from top to bottom, so they said to one another, "Let us not tear it, but cast lots for it to see whose it shall be." This was to fulfill the <u>Scripture</u> which says, "They divided my garments among them, and for my clothing they cast lots."

So the soldiers did these things, but standing by the cross of Jesus were his mother and his mother's sister, Mary the wife of Clopas, and Mary Magdalene. When Jesus saw his mother and the disciple whom he loved standing nearby, he said to his mother, "Woman, behold, your son!" Then he said to the disciple, "Behold, your mother!" And from that hour the disciple took her to his own home.

Taking care of mom. Nice touch. — PB

The Death of Jesus

After this, Jesus, knowing that all was now finished, said (to fulfill the Scripture), "I thirst." A jar full of sour wine stood there, so they put a sponge full of the sour wine on a hyssop branch and held it to his mouth. When Jesus had received the sour wine, he said, "It is finished," and he bowed his head and gave up his spirit.

What is finished? – D

Jesus' Side Is Pierced

Since it was the day of Preparation, and so that the bodies would not remain on the cross on the Sabbath (for that Sabbath was a high day), the Jews asked Pilate that their legs might be broken and that they might be taken away. So the soldiers came and broke the legs of the first, and of the other who had been crucified with him. But when they came to Jesus and saw that he was already dead, they did not break his legs.

But one of the soldiers pierced his side with a spear, and at once there came out blood and water. He who saw it has borne witness—his testimony is true, and he knows that he is telling the truth—that you also may believe. For these things took place that the Scripture might <u>be fulfilled:</u> "Not one of his bones will be broken." And again another Scripture says, "They will look on him whom they have pierced."

There it is again, another prophecy fulfilled.
— Tay

* I once had a friend that did some time as a teen for stealing a car. From the time he was arrested to the time he got out of lock up seemed like forever. He got out right before his eighteenth birthday. I remember because the judge expunged his record on his birthday. That means it was like he'd never committed the crime. It was finished and his record was clean. When Jesus dies on the cross, he's not just dying like a normal person. He's paying the price for our sin. When he says, "it is finished," he's saying he did what God sent him to do and the final part of that was his death to finally break the curse of sin. The curse is now broken - it is finished - and each of us can now have our sins forgiven.

- Uncle G.

Jesus Is Buried

After these things Joseph of Arimathea, who was a disciple of Jesus, but secretly for fear of the Jews, asked Pilate that he might take away the body of Jesus, and Pilate gave him permission. So he came and took away his body.

Nicodemus also, who earlier had come to Jesus by night, came bringing a mixture of myrrh and aloes, about seventy-five pounds in weight. So they took the body of Jesus and bound it in linen cloths with the spices, as is the burial custom of the Jews. Now in the place where he was crucified there was a garden, and in the garden a new tomb in which no one had yet been laid. So because of the Jewish day of Preparation, since the tomb was close at hand, they laid Jesus there.

That's a ton! - PB

* Kind of weird - Hey, here's an open tomb, let's use that one! - Uncle G.

CHAPTER 20

The Resurrection

Now on the first day of the week Mary Magdalene came to the tomb early, while it was still dark, and saw that the stone had been taken away from the tomb. So she ran and went to Simon Peter and the other disciple, the one whom Jesus loved, and said to them, "They have taken the Lord out of the tomb, and we do not know where they have laid him." So Peter went out with the other disciple, and they were going toward the tomb.

Possible Body Snatchers! - PB

Both of them were running together, but the other disciple outran Peter and reached the tomb first. And stooping to look in, he saw the linen cloths lying there, but he did not go in. Then Simon Peter came, following him, and went into the tomb. He saw the (linen cloths) lying there, and the face cloth, which had been on Jesus' head, not lying with the linen cloths but folded up in a place by itself.

Strange thing to leave behind if you stole the body. And someone took time to fold it? - D

Then the other disciple, who had reached the tomb first, also went in, and he saw and believed; for as yet they did not understand the Scripture, that he must rise from the dead. Then the disciples went back to their homes.

→ Believed what? That he was gone? I'm starting to believe that this is much more than a story. - PB

Jesus Appears to Mary Magdalene

But Mary stood weeping outside the tomb, and as she wept she stooped to look into the tomb. And she saw two angels in white, sitting where the body of Jesus had lain, one at the head and one at the feet.

Freaky! - V

They said to her, "Woman, why are you weeping?" She said to them, "They have taken away my Lord, and I do not know where they have laid him." Having said this, she turned around and saw Jesus standing, but she did not know that it was Jesus.

Jesus said to her, "Woman, why are you weeping? Whom are you seeking?" Supposing him to be the gardener, she said to him, "Sir, if you have carried him away, tell me where you have laid him, and I will take him away." Jesus said to her, "Mary." She turned and said to him in Aramaic, "Rabboni!" (which means Teacher).

Okay, for real, I would have fainted. - V

Jesus said to her, "Do not cling to me, for I have not yet ascended to the Father; but go to my brothers and say to them, 'I am ascending to my Father and your Father, to my God and your God.' " Mary Magdalene went and announced to the disciples, "I have seen the Lord"—and that he had said these things to her.

Did they believe her or think she'd lost it? - D

Jesus Appears to the Disciples

On the evening of that day, the first day of the week, the doors being locked where the disciples were for fear of the Jews, Jesus came and stood among them and said to them, "Peace be with you." When he had said this, he showed them his hands and his side.

So, did he just like poof through the door? - D

Then the disciples were glad when they saw the Lord. Jesus said to them again, "Peace be with you. As the Father has sent me, even so I am sending you." And when he had said this, he breathed on them and said to them, "Receive the Holy Spirit. If you forgive the sins of any, they are forgiven them; if you withhold forgiveness from any, it is withheld."

Did he have bad breath from being dead? - PB

Seems like a little too much power to give a person. - D

Jesus and Thomas

Now Thomas, one of the Twelve, called the Twin, was not with them when Jesus came. So the other disciples told him, "We have seen the Lord." But he said to them, "Unless I see in his hands the mark of the nails, and place my finger into the mark of the nails, and place my hand into his side, I will never believe."

Same thing I would've said. - D

Rises from the dead and goes through doors! Massive skills! - PB

Eight days later, his disciples were inside again, and Thomas was with them. Although the doors were locked, Jesus came and stood among them and said,

"Peace be with you." Then he said to Thomas, "Put your finger here, and see my hands; and put out your hand, and place it in my side. Do not disbelieve, but believe." Thomas answered him, "My Lord and my God!" Jesus said to him, "Have you believed because you have seen me? <u>Blessed</u> are those who have not seen and yet have believed."

I think that's me. I believe. — Tay

The Purpose of This Book

Now Jesus did many other signs in the presence of the disciples, which are not written in this book; but these are written so that you may believe that Jesus is the Christ, the Son of God, and that by believing you may have life in <u>his name.</u>

I hope everyone reading this book decides to believe in Jesus and gets to have eternal life just like it says here. — Tay

CHAPTER 21

Jesus Appears to Seven Disciples

After this Jesus revealed himself again to the disciples by the Sea of Tiberias, and he revealed himself in this way. Simon Peter, Thomas (called the Twin), Nathanael of Cana in Galilee, the sons of Zebedee, and two others of his disciples were together.

Simon Peter said to them, "I am going fishing." They said to him, "We will go with you." They went out and got into the boat, but that night they caught nothing. *My grandpa would've caught something. He always catches fish when I go with him. — V*

Just as day was breaking, Jesus stood on the shore; yet the disciples did not know that it was Jesus. Jesus said to them, "Children, do you have any fish?" They answered him, "No."

He said to them, "Cast the net on the right side of the boat, and you will find some." So they cast it, and now they were not able to haul it in, because of the quantity of fish. *Can I take this guy fishing with me? - D*

It seems weird to put clothes on to jump in the water. - V

That disciple whom Jesus loved therefore said to Peter, "It is the Lord!" When Simon Peter heard that it was the Lord, he put on his outer garment, for he was stripped for work, and threw himself into the sea.

The other disciples came in the boat, dragging the net full of fish, for they were not far from the land, but about a hundred yards off. When they got out on land, they saw a charcoal fire in place, with fish laid out on it, and bread.

Jesus said to them, "Bring some of the fish that you have just caught." So Simon Peter went aboard and hauled the net ashore, full of large fish, 153 of them. And although there were so many, the net was not torn. Jesus said to them, "Come and have breakfast."

I think this is so amazing. Jesus was just killed, came back from the dead and is now making breakfast for his followers. The son of God making breakfast. Wow! - Tay

Now none of the disciples dared ask him, "Who are you?" They knew it was the Lord. Jesus came and took the bread and gave it to them, and so with the fish. This was now the third time that Jesus was revealed to the disciples after he was raised from the dead.

Jesus and Peter

When they had finished breakfast, Jesus said to Simon Peter, "Simon, son of John, do you love me more than these?" He said to him, "Yes, Lord; you know

Good question after he denied him a few days ago. - D

that I love you." He said to him, "Feed my lambs." He said to him a second time, "Simon, son of John, do you love me?" He said to him, "Yes, Lord; you know that I love you." He said to him, "Tend my sheep."

He said to him the third time, "Simon, son of John, do you love me?" Peter was grieved because he said to him the third time, "Do you love me?" and he said to him, "Lord, you know everything; you know that I love you." Jesus said to him, "Feed my sheep.

I get it — denied him 3 times — has to say he loves him 3 times. — PB

reading Jesus story like this kind of opened my eyes. He's easy to love. — V

"Truly, truly, I say to you, when you were young, you used to dress yourself and walk wherever you wanted, but when you are old, you will stretch out your hands, and another will dress you and carry you where you do not want to go." (This he said to show by what kind of death he was to glorify God.) And after saying this he said to him, "Follow me."

Not complicated. I think I'm pretty much ready to follow him. — D

Jesus and the Beloved Apostle
Peter turned and saw the disciple whom Jesus loved following them, the one who had been reclining at table close to him and had said, "Lord, who is it that is going to betray you?"

When Peter saw him, he said to Jesus, "Lord, what about this man?" Jesus said to him, "If it is my will that he remain until I come, what is that to you? You follow me!" So the saying spread abroad among the brothers that this disciple was not to die; yet Jesus did not say to him that he was not to die, but, "If it is my will that he remain until I come, what is that to you?"

I love that. Jesus says what is that to you? That is very cool. — V

This is the disciple who is bearing witness about these things, and who has written these things, and we know that his testimony is true. Now there are also many other things that Jesus did. Were every one of them to be written, I suppose that the world itself could not contain the books that would be written.

I'd like to read them.
— Tay

WHAT ABOUT YOU?

NOW IS YOUR CHANCE TO MAKE A <u>CRUCIAL DECISION</u> ABOUT
YOUR LIFE AND YOUR FUTURE.

Best decision I've ever made!
— Tay

Jesus asked an important question when He was here on Earth:

"Who do YOU say that I am?"

WHO DO YOU SAY JESUS IS?

Is He the son of God? Did He live without sin? Did He pay the penalty for Your sin, breaking the curse? Did He rise again from the dead?

He was either crazy to die when He could have easily avoided it or He was and is the son of God.

Who do You say Jesus is?
   a. Son of God who lived a sinless life and died to pay for my sin
   b. Crazy peasant preacher who died for nothing
   c. _____

The next most important question is:

WHO ARE YOU?

Are you a sinner who has inherited the curse placed on all people? Is your sin keeping you from God? What is your eternal destination, heaven or hell?

The Bible says in John 3:18 that if you don't believe in who Jesus is and what He has done for you, then right now you stand condemned to an eternity in hell.

Who are you?

a. Under the curse, condemned to hell without Jesus

b. Doing fine without God and not worried about when I die

c. _____

SO, WHAT WILL YOU DO?

Jesus said, "Come Follow Me."

If you agree with God, (confess) that you are a sinner who desperately needs your sins paid for with the ultimate sacrifice, there is good news.

In the Bible, in the book of 1 John, God says: "If you confess your sins, He is faithful and just to forgive you."

God can forgive you based on the sacrifice of Jesus.

In the Bible, in the book of Romans God says:

"If you confess with your mouth Jesus is Lord and believe in your heart that God raised Him from the dead, you will be saved."

It doesn't matter who you are or what you've done. You don't have to clean up your life first. God is passionately in love with you and is waiting with open arms for you to run to him. You can make that decision right now, wherever you are and whatever you're doing.

How to Make Things Right With God (and get to Heaven)

Okay, so when I started reading and making notes I thought it would just be fun. Now, I'm pretty much ready to say I believe. I need forgiveness and want to follow Jesus. Crazy - D

1. Confess to God you are a sinner.
   - ☐ SAY "God, I admit I'm a sinner"

2. Tell Him you believe Jesus died to pay the penalty for your sin and rose from the dead to give you new life.
   - ☐ SAY "I believe Jesus' death on the cross paid the penalty for my sin and his rising from the dead gives me new life"

3. Tell Him that you trust Jesus to forgive you and give you a fresh start.
   - ☐ SAY "God, I trust you to forgive my sins and give me a fresh start"

4. Ask Him to come and live in you through His spirit.
   - ☐ SAY "God, please come and live in me by your Holy Spirit"

5. Commit your life to following Him and His ways.
   - ☐ SAY "I commit my life to follow Your ways, not my ways. Please help me do that. Amen."

Sometimes this isn't easy. It means your life has to change from doing things the way you've always done them to doing them more like Jesus would do them. Things like showing love when you just want to punch someone or talk trash about them, choosing to do what's right even when everyone else is doing what's wrong (that can be lonely, trust me), putting others' needs before your needs that one is very tough for me. I'm kind of selfish. The good news is the Holy Spirit now lives inside of you (sounds kind of freaky when you think about it) and He helps you to follow Jesus. — Tay

If you decided to follow Jesus today, the Bible says your name is now written in the Lamb's Book of Life.

Sign your name below with today's date so you can remember the day you decided to follow Jesus.

_____   _____

Child of God/Follower of Jesus (Your Name)   Today's Date

All these years of going to church, and I've never actually
prayed a prayer to have my sins forgiven and commit to
being a follower of Jesus. Today is my day.

– V

FIRST STEPS

- Contact the person who gave you the Life Book and let them know of your decision. They will be very happy for you!

- Ask the person who gave you the Life Book to help you get a complete Bible to read.

- Go to church with the person who gave you the Life Book. This will help you in your new life of following Jesus.

- Read a little bit of your Bible every day.

- Talk to God every day. Let him know your concerns, your worries, and ask for His help and direction in your new life.

- Find friends who follow Jesus.

- Tell others about your new decision to follow Jesus Christ.

HELP!

THIS SECTION IS FOR EVERYONE WHO HAS EVER WISHED THEY COULD SIT DOWN WITH GOD AND ASK HIM ABOUT PROBLEMS IN THEIR LIFE. YOU MAY NOT BE STRUGGLING RIGHT NOW, BUT MAYBE A FRIEND NEEDS YOUR HELP. WE HAVE PROVIDED SOME PASSAGES FROM THE BIBLE THAT WILL HOPEFULLY HELP YOU THROUGH AND GIVE YOU SOME GUIDANCE.

RELATIONSHIPS AND SEX

Am I really in love?

Love is patient and kind; love does not envy or boast; it is not arrogant or rude. It does not insist on its own way; it is not irritable or resentful; it does not rejoice at wrongdoing, but rejoices with the truth. Love bears all things, believes all things, hopes all things, endures all things.

(1 Corinthians 13:4-7)

I haven't really met many guys who look at love this way. Most of the guys around here are totally selfish, and all most of them do is brag about how great they are. So is that really love? Maybe not! —V

God Reserves Sex for Marriage?

"Therefore a man shall leave his father and mother and hold fast to his wife, and the two shall become one flesh." (Ephesians 5:31)

What is all this talk about slaves and sanctification? Are we still talking about sex? —PB

For this is the will of God, your sanctification: that you abstain from sexual immorality; that each one of you know how to control his own body in holiness and honor, not in the passion of lust like the Gentiles who do not know God; (1 Thessalonians 4:3-5)

Do you not know that if you present yourselves to anyone as obedient <u>slaves</u>, you are <u>slaves</u> of the one whom you obey, either of sin, which leads to death, or of obedience, which leads to righteousness? (Romans 6:16)

So many of my friends think they are ready for sex. But what do we really know? Are we ready for babies, for STD's, and for broken hearts? I have a really good friend who thought she and her boyfriend were ready for sex, so they went ahead and had it. She thought it was love, but found out pretty fast that it wasn't. She gave up her heart to a guy who didn't really care, and dumped her a few weeks later. But then she figured that since she had already had sex once, it wasn't a big deal to do it again... and again...and again. That is what being a "slave" means — she couldn't stop herself, even though she hated herself more and more every time she had sex with another guy. That's why I think God saves sex for marriage. — Tay

How far is too far?*

Flee from sexual immorality. Every other sin a person commits is outside the body, but the sexually immoral person sins against his own body.
(1 Corinthians 6:18)

*Kids always ask me how far is too far. I tell them that even thinking about sex is too far. I was a teenage boy once and I know how their minds work. You think you can stop with just kissing, but then you go to the next step. Before long, you've already had sex, and you don't even remember making a choice to go that far - it just happened. Don't even let your mind go there, and then the next step never comes at you. God's plan is for you to wait until you're married.

-Uncle G.

But sexual immorality and all impurity or covetousness must not even be named among you, as is proper among saints. (Ephesians 5:3)

Do not desire her beauty in your heart, and do not let her capture you with her eyelashes; (Proverbs 6:25)

But I say to you that everyone who looks at a woman with lustful intent has already committed adultery with her in his heart. (Matthew 5:28)

I've had sex, now I feel guilty...

Therefore, if anyone is in Christ, he is a new creation. The old has passed away; behold, the new has come. (II Corinthians 5:17)

If we confess our sins, he is faithful and just to forgive us our sins and to cleanse us from all unrighteousness. (I John 1:9)

It's good to know that even when we've messed up, God gives us a clean slate.
— V

Wait a minute - if I even think about doing stuff with a girl, its the same as if I already did it? That's not right! I'm a gamer - I understand the difference between reality and fantasy. If the game I'm playing is about killing people, it doesn't mean I've really killed anyone - its NOT REAL! So how is thinking about sex like having sex?
-D

FRIENDS / PEER PRESSURE

Submit yourselves therefore to God. Resist the devil, and he will flee from you. (James 4:7)

No temptation has overtaken you that is not common to man. God is faithful, and he will not let you be tempted beyond your ability, but with the temptation he will also provide the way of escape, that you may be able to endure it. (1 Corinthians 10:13)

Do not be deceived: "Bad company ruins good morals." Wake up from your drunken stupor, as is right, and do not go on sinning. For some have no knowledge of God. I say this to your shame. (1 Corinthians 15:33-34)

You shall not fall in with the many to do evil, nor shall you bear witness in a lawsuit, siding with the many, so as to pervert justice, nor shall you be partial to a poor man in his lawsuit. (Exodus 23:2-3)

Do not enter the path of the wicked, and do not walk in the way of the evil. Avoid it; do not go on it; turn away from it and pass on. For they cannot sleep unless they have done wrong; they are robbed of sleep unless they have <u>made someone stumble</u>. (Proverbs 4:14-16)

But when Herod's birthday came, the daughter of Herodias danced before the company and pleased Herod, so that he promised with an oath to give her whatever she might ask. Prompted by her mother, she said, "Give me the head of John the Baptist here on a platter." And the king was sorry, but because of his oaths and his guests he commanded it to be given. He sent and had John beheaded in the prison, (Matthew 14:6-10)

But they were urgent, demanding with loud cries that he should be crucified. And their voices prevailed. 24So Pilate decided that their demand should be granted. (Luke 23:23-24)

> I kind of realized something the other day after watching how my friends act. All they care about is what other people think. I hate to admit it, but I guess I'm kind of like them. It's like I let everyone else's opinion run my life. Doesn't really make any sense now that I think about it. It's still hard. But I'm thinking about finding some different friends that pressure me to do good stuff instead of bad stuff. Not sure if that's the answer, but I think it'll help.
> —PB

My dad always says "Misery loves company"— people who pressure you into doing bad things are usually just looking for someone to share the blame or get down in the dirt with them!
— Tay

SELF IMAGE / SELF-ESTEEM

I praise you, for I am fearfully and wonderfully made. Wonderful are your works; my soul knows it very well. My frame was not hidden from you, when I was being made in secret, intricately woven in the depths of the earth. Your eyes saw my unformed substance; in your book were written, every one of them, the days that were formed for me, when as yet there was none of them.
(Psalm 139:14-16)

So we do not lose heart. Though our outer self is wasting away, our inner self is being renewed day by day. (2 Corinthians 4:16)

Or do you not know that your body is a temple of the Holy Spirit within you, whom you have from God? You are not your own, for you were bought with a price. So glorify God in your body. (1 Corinthians 6:19-20)

I appeal to you therefore, brothers, by the mercies of God, to present your bodies as a living sacrifice, holy and acceptable to God, which is your spiritual worship. (Romans 12:1)

But the Lord said to Samuel, "Do not look on his appearance or on the height of his stature, because I have rejected him. For the Lord sees not as man sees: man looks on the outward appearance, but the Lord looks on the heart."
(1 Samuel 16:7)

But he gives more grace. Therefore it says, "God opposes the proud, but gives grace to the humble." (James 4:6)

Jesus said, "Whoever receives this child in my name receives me, and whoever receives me receives him who sent me. For he who is least among you all is the one who is great." (Luke 9:48)

My friends face so many issues that all come back to self-image. Steroids, eating disorders, crazy diets, cutting, arrogance, bullying...the list goes on. I wish everyone would see that God made each one of us special and just accept who they really are. — Tay

I always used to think I was fat. When I was in 6th grade, I used to make myself throw up all the time to help lose weight. The youth leader at my church found me in the bathroom one day and talked to me about how God thinks I'm beautiful and my body is like His temple or something He is really proud of. She told me to focus on being beautiful on the inside. It sounded cheesy, but after a few years, I started to see that I wasn't fat, and in fact, God had done a pretty good job when He made me!
—V

DEPRESSION / WORRY

Why are you cast down, O my soul, and why are you in turmoil within me? Hope in God; for I shall again praise him, my salvation (Psalm 42:5)

Trust in the Lord with all your heart, and do not lean on your own understanding. In all your ways acknowledge him, and he will make straight your paths. (Proverbs 3:5-6)

May the God of hope fill you with all joy and peace in believing, so that by the power of the Holy Spirit you may abound in hope. (Romans 15:13)

Rejoice in the Lord always; again I will say, Rejoice. Let your reasonableness be known to everyone. The Lord is at hand; do not be anxious about anything, but in everything by prayer and supplication with thanksgiving let your requests be made known to God. And the peace of God, which surpasses all understanding, will guard your hearts and your minds in Christ Jesus. (Philippians 4:4-7)

We are afflicted in every way, but not crushed; perplexed, but not driven to despair; persecuted, but not forsaken; struck down, but not destroyed; So we do not lose heart. Though our outer self is wasting away, our inner self is being renewed day by day. (2 Corinthians 4:8-9, 16)

but they who wait for the Lord shall renew their strength; they shall mount up with wings like eagles; they shall run and not be weary; they shall walk and not faint. (Isaiah 40:31)

So people in the bible were depressed too?
Good to know I'm not the only one!
 — V

I have trouble with this. I trust God, really I do. But it's so hard to not
worry about things. My mom is amazing with this. She has faced some
really hard times in her life, but she is always so peaceful and doesn't
stress out about it. I know she prays all the time and tells anyone who
will listen to her that God has been good to her. It's just amazing to me
that she can be so positive at times when everyone else falls into massive
depression.
 — Tay

I don't know that I would say I've ever been "depressed." There are
times I feel really overwhelmed and don't want to think about things
anymore — that's when I go online and play video games even more
than I do now. There are times in life when I just get so tired of
dealing with garbage, so I like this verse — it would be cool to fly like
a bird — high above all the problems in this world.
 — D

MY NOTES

In all things I have shown you that by working hard in this way we must help the weak and remember the words of the Lord Jesus, how he himself said, 'It is more **blessed** to **give** than to **receive**.'"

Acts 20:35

WHO WILL YOU GIVE
THE LIFE BOOK TO?

SHARE YOUR LIFE BOOK STORY

thelifebook.com/share

WANT TO BRING THE LIFE BOOK TO YOUR AREA?

Ask your youth leader to go to thelifebook.com/youth-leaders

WANT A DIGITAL COPY OF THE LIFE BOOK?

FREE and downloadable...Go to thelifebook.com/read

LIKE US ON FACEBOOK

facebook.com/thelifebookmovement